Praise

'I couldn't put this book dow
myth-busting style. The book moves quickly and
stays focused on specific areas, so it's easy to dip in
and out. It's also practical: you can look at a myth,
read it and apply what you've learned. It's very
reader-friendly.'
— **Liz Allison**, People and Culture Director,
Hamilton Court FX

'When I began reading *Untangle Your Sales*, I didn't
know what to expect. I often find business books
dry and stuffed with obvious statements aimed at
people with a variety of problems that look nothing
like mine. As I read *Untangle Your Sales*, it was like
Lynne and Martin had been watching me for years,
studying my progress, and had decided it really
was time to help me out. In their own quirky way,
they demonstrate a genuine understanding of an
entrepreneur's journey from start-up, when passion
and enthusiasm drive the business on, to the point
when the need for a more structured approach to
sales kicks in. This is one of the few books I wish I'd
read earlier.'
— **Tony Stein**, Chief Executive, Healthcare
Management Solutions

'The world is changing more rapidly than ever, and, for a business leader employing a sales team, it can be easy to become entangled in endless "how to" books and seminars. In *Untangle Your Sales* Lynne and Martin debunk corporate myths, with their people-centred, down-to-earth approach. Read and apply this book to bring a new energy to the sales within your business.'

— **Paul Hargreaves**, CEO, Cotswold Fayre, B Corp Ambassador, speaker, and author of *Forces for Good*

'Martin and Lynne tackle the pressing question of how you can carry out the "dirty business" of sales effectively yet purposefully – aligned with your own beliefs and core purpose. As the owner of a small business that has grown organically, this book spoke my language and spoke to the very challenges I was facing when it came to selling. A must-read for any leader who feels daunted by the prospect of tackling those dreaded sales knots.'

— **Dave Vann**, Managing Director, ABA | Building brands with purpose

'I have never managed to read any business book all the way through – until now. I found *Untangle Your Sales* engaging, thought-provoking and exhilarating. It has made me rethink some of the ways of working within my own business, and I have found myself returning to the book and digging back into the sales myths. Martin and Lynne have certainly managed to reboot my inner energy, and I am now relooking at how we can excite our internal sales teams, clients, trade customers and consumers.'

— **Mandy Willmore**, Managing Director, Powermed Plus

'A brilliant guide to sales, specifically the parts people don't usually tell you about. It's superb and busts all the classic myths we are told. I wish I could have read this earlier.'

— **Rob Turner**, Group CEO, Kinetic

Lynne Kennedy
and Martin Knowles

Untangle Your

Sales

The business owner's
guide to making
sales growth simple

R^ethink

First published in Great Britain in 2021
by Rethink Press (www.rethinkpress.com)

© Copyright Martin Knowles and Lynne Kennedy

Contents

Preface   1

Introduction   5

PART ONE Sales Myths   35

Introduction: Sales Myths   37

1   Sales Myth #1: Sales Is About
Winners And Losers   41

2   Sales Myth #2: My Ten Biggest Customers
Are My Most Important   47

3   Sales Myth #3: We Can Absorb Cost
Price Increases This Year   55

4   Sales Myth #4: We Can Recoup Today's
Discount On The Next Deal   61

5   Sales Myth #5: My Sales Team Will Give Me
Honest Feedback If Something's Going Wrong   69

6   Sales Myth #6: I Need A Hungry Sales Team   79

7   Sales Myth #7: You Can Kick A Sales Person
And They Will Bounce Back Immediately   85

8   Sales Myth #8: With Sales You Get
What You Measure   91

9   Sales Myth #9: Sales People Are All
A Bit Untrustworthy   97

10   Sales Myth #10: I Need A Sales
Person Urgently   107

11   Sales Myth #11: I Can't Sell. Can You Help?   113

12   Sales Myth #12: The CRM System
Will Tell Me That   117

13   Sales Myth #13: I Know I Need
To Be On Facebook   123

14   Sales Myth #14: Customers?
That's Sales' Job   127

15   Sales Myth #15: We'd Be Alright If
It Wasn't For Customers   133

16   Sales Myth #16: Couldn't We Double Our
Sales Just By Improving Conversion Rates?   137

Conclusion   143

PART TWO Bringing Solutions To Life   145

Introduction: Solutions   147

17 Why Do We Do This?   149

18 Can You Help Me Get The
    Customers I Deserve?   163

19 Who Are My Most Important Customers?   173

20 How Do I Prove The Return On
    Investment (ROI) For This?   183

21 Can You Help Me Become
    Confident In Sales?   195

22 How Do I Choose Between
    Hunters And Farmers?   205

23 How Do I Recruit Great Sales People?   213

24 How Do I Get The Best Out Of
    New Sales People?   227

25 What's A Sales Culture And Can I Have One? 235

26 How Do I Build A High-performing
    Sales Team?   245

27 What's My Customer Journey?   257

28 What Are The Best Sales KPIs?   267

29 How Do I Get The Best Price For My
   Products And Services?   275

30 Can You Help Me Build An Efficient Sales
   Funnel... Or Do I Mean Sales Process?   285

Conclusion   297

Acknowledgements   305

The Authors   307

Preface

The year 2020 knocked the business world off its axis. Some industries were as good as closed, while those involved in home delivery and remote working saw business boom. Organisations of all sizes had to find new ways of reaching customers; some of which will fade in short order, while others become the 'new normal'. In this new world, has the nature of sales changed?

The simple answer is yes. And no.

Yes, because the Covid pandemic changed business and personal relationships by provoking intense emotions: feelings of fear as the disease spread; feelings of helplessness as we watched the economy close; the practical emotions triggered by being overwhelmed with home schooling, sanitising and keeping our families safe. Just as our grandparents regaled us with tales of post-war hardship, we'll be telling our offspring about lockdown. 'We were literally locked in our homes for six weeks,' and, 'Your grandad had a mask that made him look like Darth Vader.'

Yet no, because the fundamentals of good sales practice haven't shifted. Examples of figuring out your most important customers, controlling customer discounts and building a great team remain essential best practice.

Our changing environment has changed our motives and beliefs. One survey after another shows that consumers and customers expect better of business. Businesses with true purpose at their heart are more successful both in building brand and attracting talent.

People in sales have a unique position. With their external focus, they are the eyes of a business and uniquely placed to act as the catalyst for bringing together supplier and customer in this new era of co-creation.

Our economy is shot to pieces and our national debt racing ahead with numbers we can barely conceive. For those running small businesses, already over-loaded diaries have been lengthened with insolvent customers and cashflow crises.

In today's world we need to double our efforts to sell, and this book offers countless practical tools to do that. Simultaneously, we need to demonstrate trust, empathy and togetherness to attract people who want to spend with us and recommend us. The theme throughout this book is exactly this: to build a sustainable sales capability.

Those who embrace the role of sales in this way can likely identify a commercial world in which we truly build back better. They will be the leaders who come to love sales because they know it helps them excite customers, build great teams and give more to the community that surrounds them. They're the ones with sales in their soul.

Introduction

Tangled

Hedges don't move.

Not of their own volition. He knew that. And unless he'd accidentally followed the White Rabbit down a bunny hole and the Queen of Hearts was about to order his early and unwarranted demise, then something was badly wrong.

These hedges were moving. Every turn he took in his increasingly frantic search for the exit was met with a blockade of evergreen. There appeared to be no going back, nor did there appear to be any way out. Do hedges menace? These did.

Have you noticed how supposedly benign parts of your business move without invitation?

It had started gently enough. He'd found himself jogging within the confines of what felt like a puzzle. Yew hedges rose way above his head, ancient living battalions standing in formation, saluting an ancient magic only they remembered. It had begun with certainty, at least once he'd realised that he was lost and somehow entombed at the centre. How had that happened?

He trusted his instincts. He knew how to find north using the sun to shadow-line and he was an endurance, long-distance obsessed cyclist, used to keeping his body and brain working long after both were pleading for mercy and wanting to quit. He was no quitter.

He prided himself on being able to jump on his bike at the end of a monster day and pedal 40 miles before the siren of supper and family called him back. His family understood that without this pressure valve he brought the squirrels home in his head instead of dumping them at the roadside as he slogged up another incline.

What's your release valve?

He wasn't easily spooked. Surviving numerous close encounters with Chelsea tractors had taught him to remain calm and thoughtful when it looked as though he was about to have a layer of his skin removed by a wing mirror. It had also taught him that retaliation, whether verbal or via semaphore, would almost always make things worse. Seventy-three kilos of skinny human armed with a carbon-fibre bike and a spare inner tube was never going to win the battle with a particulate-breathing, 4x4, two-tonne dragon.

But his instincts, or maybe his reality, were failing. Certainly, his decision-making was falling apart. Every turn, every reversal, every attempt to push through the green sentinels rather than obeying their rules left him exactly as before: lost in a world that was inextricably tightening around him.

So now he was spooked. Very spooked.

How often are you spooked by the need to make quick decisions without data?

His sense of time had long since deserted him and using the sun to find a point on any compass rapidly becomes no more than a party trick when the trap you're snared in has deliberately swallowed your illumination.

He was certain he'd arrived here in daylight, but all he glimpsed overhead was purple-tinged twilight with skeins of ink-black clouds dominating his vision. There must have been sunlight somewhere as each storm cloud was outlined with a tiny edge of deep gold along its right-hand flank. Daylight's last hurrah before night descended. Maybe his too?

Can you still find true north for your business?

That's when the movement became obvious – or maybe that's when he noticed that he felt like prey. As his view diminished to shadowed outlines and his hearing replaced his vital sense of sight, he began to accept that this was not a game.

At weekends he raced his bike. He knew how adrenaline felt as it kicked in and coursed through his body, priming him to punch out from the start and outsprint his competition. He recognised the butterflies in his stomach that had turned up uninvited. For once they weren't flying in formation but signalling danger and the need to move fast: to get out. As was the roar of his heart in his ears. But how?

How do you interpret the warning signs and symptoms that appear to be telling you that all is not well? Can you trust that pedalling faster will be the answer?

Yew. Wasn't that what was planted in graveyards? Twisted and gnarled, leaning away from prevailing winds, silently marking the passing of centuries and of life and expectations. Was it just to keep the sheep away as some said or was it something deeper, older, wiser or more dangerous? Wasn't it poisonous? Why was he caught within its lair?

Run! Every sinew in his body and the very core of his brain screamed. Run! Now!

And he did. Pushing forwards, his left hand faced outwards to skim the edge of the trees and provide some sense of movement and equilibrium. His eyes desperately scanned the darkness, searching in vain for a pinpoint of light to fix on and confirm that he could still see. He ran. Blind.

Random turns of left and right would move him away from the centre of the trap but his mounting terror totally disrupted his reason. The overwhelming silence was punctuated only by his occasional barks of fear as his hand caught at sharp branches. His hands and face burned as though repeatedly nicked by a scalpel point as he scraped and bounced along the steely tips of the branches.

What's foremost in your business: the overwhelming adrenaline of running, or defining the right track to follow?

He came to a stop, gasping for breath and his legs burning hotter than any hill climb. Once his lungs calmed and he could hear beyond his own panting he realised that he was still intact and gave silent thanks.

Stop. Breathe. Think.

How many decisions have you made in blind panic as a reaction to moments of pressure or terror? How many have you gone on to regret?

He felt a breeze. In fact, he heard the rustle of leaves first and then felt the gentle movement. Was he closer to the outer boundaries of the maze and nearer to freedom now? Think.

He paid no attention to the gentle tickle on his neck as he scanned about in the darkness trying to work out what to do next, nor did he notice what was happening at his feet.

Isn't it often things at a low level that trip you up?

At an unnatural speed, tendrils shot out of the yew all around him. Tiny, twitching, searching. Indiscernible in the dark, they gathered pace as though scenting their prey. Then they began to twine and twist around him.

Distracted, he brushed off the first few thinking that they were midnight insects looking for an easy meal, but after a couple of mindless swipes he was fully alert. Cold, fleshy fingers of growth were probing his skin and wrapping themselves around him. Malevolently inquisitive, they probed, searched and then began to coil.

He frantically peeled them off his face and pulled them out of his ears, keeping his hands moving fast to avoid being caught. His stomach retched as he felt one crawl across his scalp and make for his forehead. Others moved across his shoulders and chest as he fought and peeled them off as best he could.

How do you hold back tomorrow's problems when today's problems are trying to choke you?

Terror mounting but not daring to scream for fear of opening his mouth and letting them in, his brain screamed. Run! Only as he hit the ground with a sickening crunch of shoulder muscle and bone did he realise that he'd ignored his feet and was shackled.

Now he screamed.

Have you noticed how business can make you feel trapped? How the reasons you started this crazy maze seem to ensnare you and wrap themselves around you, one tendril at a time?

Bolt upright now. Pitch black. Wide awake with every sense on immediate high alert. Staring frantically for a point of focus to regain his equilibrium. Listening for clues to his sudden disturbance and finding none. His skin damp with sweat but corpse-cold to the touch. At least he was in bed.

The maze. A repeating nightmare.

What keeps you awake at night?

Just how had his world contracted to such a strangled fixation?

The leap

His father had been fit when he was alive. A long-distance walker, thinking nothing of waking up in the dark to yomp up another high peak to share a sandwich and a sunrise with his friends at the summit. An ex-government man with his entire working life dedicated to making thousands of micro-decisions to keep an entire department ticking along and a massive budget predictably on track.

They'd laughed together when Dad retired. Faced with no more complicated a decision than how to spend his morning, Dad's faffing and debate about which decision was preferable could extract a good hour from every day. Retirement and decision-making had quickly become nemeses.

Decisions were eventually made and Dad did eventually get moving. Not unlike that crisp innocuous Sunday morning when he'd bounced out of the house to play tennis. Full of energy and enthusiasm for spending a morning with his other retired buddies, he had tales to tell of his recent sixty-eighth birthday that had involved cake and more candles than one person could reasonably deal with.

How can you be certain that the next step you take will improve your business situation rather than exacerbate the problem?

Shaking himself from his reflections about his father, he returned to the here and now. He was being eaten alive by indecision too. It had all appeared to be such an easy choice. No risk. Immediate returns guaranteed. Success, riches and bragging rights to go with it. Really? Had he been that gullible, or just that lost?

Once upon a time it had been different.

He wasn't sure whether it had been better – he'd forgotten the real details, but definitely different. He'd led an important department, been entrusted to develop others around him and challenged to succeed. He'd had a payroll number, entitlement to a pension should he make it to retirement, access to an 'HR partner' (whatever one of those was) and the trappings of corporate achievement.

It was probably an illusion, but in his fleeting reminiscences it seemed to him that some mornings the most significant decision he'd had to make was whether to have cappuccino or latte for breakfast. In stark contrast he now let lunch slip past him unnoticed and sat alone well into the night staring at an omnipotent cursor tracking the search for magic that eluded him. If emitted blue light was really as dangerous as some suggested then maybe technology would have the last laugh.

His devotion to company town hall meetings and awaydays had waned quickly when he'd realised that the price for his salary and shares was increasingly large portions of his soul. He'd balked at the politics and positioning that went on around him and with him. He'd increasingly resisted the requirement to 'play the game' and somewhere along the line paid a price for that in the projects his team were afforded and the meetings he was increasingly left off the electronic invite for.

He'd been restless for a while before it happened, but the long-distance phone call he'd received while his dad should have been bouncing around the tennis court crystallised his intent and desire for escape. The paramedics had apparently done all they could but the heart attack was massive and his dad had been dead before he hit the court. Apparently, they were to be comforted that he'd felt nothing.

By the time he stood beside the coffin, it was no longer a surprise, but the predictable and inevitable still shook him to the core. He watched with heartbroken distraction the familiar and unfamiliar faces mourn his dad's passing with a variety of platitudes replacing a straightforward but unutterable, 'I'm sorry he's dead.'

Distraught, he played his own future in fast-forward, and with a clarity that both disturbed and thrilled him, he recognised his overwhelming need to be free. It was his moment of no return.

Often a bolt from the blue outside of work forces someone to question purpose. It may be having children, or the bitter-sweet day they finally leave home. Sometimes it's the death of a loved one or a close shave with an unexpected and unwelcome medical diagnosis but it's enough to trigger the decision: the work I'm doing just doesn't have enough meaning for me.

What was your trigger?

The shed

And so, he stepped off the company conveyor belt and into his shed. This was where the magic began and it consumed him. Not like now. This was the genuine article. The glints of diamonds shot through with rainbows, the laughter and thrill of success marked by a silent and wonky one-person jig and a celebratory coffee break sitting on the doorstep. Long nights and early mornings accompanied by illegible doodles in a notebook where he'd emptied his brain of new ideas so that he could get back to sleep – experiments, refinements and resilience all marking his pursuit of freedom.

For a while it worked. He grew confident. Got busier. Achieved success. For a while he cast his own spells, dream-weaving ideas into reality and marvelling at the pace and scale he achieved. He was delighted with his creation and the company he kept, not minding that he was last to leave, groping his way to his eight-year-old car across a midnight-lit carpark, or that he was first to arrive, releasing the alarm from its ever-watchful state as he hustled about getting ready for the day. Gaps in his knowledge were plugged with energy and movement and a little wishful thinking. He was accelerating to freedom.

Friends openly admired his determination, his courage and his success, albeit from the comfort of their payroll and leased cars. A bit envious of his world as they saw it, but safe in the knowledge they'd never make the same leap. Acquaintances stopped to share stories, pick his brains about their own woes, or guardedly calibrate their own place in the world against him – often finding they came up short.

For a good while it worked.

But then it ceased. Not like the gentle impercep-tive shifting of a tide, giving him time to adjust and accept a new way of being, but as an immediate 'Error

Message: system crash and reboot required' tidal wave.

How many times have you ridden the rollercoaster of learning?

There followed a significant period of denial. His, in the main. He was careful to preserve his pretence of normality at first. In the past he'd always been able to reboot his energy, his progress, his success and freedom. This would be the same, wouldn't it?

'Try harder, do faster, keep moving – the magic is there,' powering him from moment to moment via increasingly urgent decisions. This time wasn't the same though. Now, he was trapped and totally tangled...

On a scale of one to ten, how strong is the buzz for you right now?

It had appeared an easy switch: from corporate employee to corporate supplier. He'd made the most of his connections and introductions to inveigle his way back into his own business and provide the very products he'd used without a flicker of thought back in the day he'd owned a dusted, clean desk and a chair with four matching feet.

He'd said goodbye to the shed nine years and three months ago, swapping the spiders, an intermittent electric supply and late-grabbed lunches for a serviced office offering pretty much the same experience but for a much higher commitment and much less access to daylight.

Staff had joined him. A small gang committed to the same ideals as him, but with slightly more surety of being paid at the end of each month. Everyone shared everything – their snacks, their ideas, their customer stories and their progress. Everyone knew where everyone stood without the need for long meetings or emails and for a while osmosis did appear to be a phenomenon upon which his dreams could flourish.

How sure are you your team will tell you if it's about to go wrong?

He struggled to recount how he had felt then, before the shadows subsumed him, but he was pretty certain that optimism and purpose had been high on the list and his family had shared that with him on the nights he made it home before the midnight radio pips welcomed another working day.

Busyness had become an indelible mark branded across his entire life.

Do you still have the energy of the shed?

Building

His momentum had pace and his staff had contagious energy. Like a dragon-boat drummer he guided his business, working to the inaudible repetitive beat of a desire to succeed in the world as his team paddled forward with an instinctive choreography that astonished him.

Everyone was learning new tricks – some improvised to accommodate a lack of process behind the scenes; others acquired new skills needed within the team. No one minded when days didn't go according to plan, nor did anyone moan when they realised there wasn't a plan and he was making most of it up on the fly.

Is it possible to make it when you 'can't sell'?

It was a joy and an adventure, and he was hooked.

He had learned that staff numbers, the budget he claimed to have influence over and the revenue he invoiced were just boastful moments to be savoured or even embellished, but never relied upon.

He had also learned the unadorned fact that cash ruled – how it ebbed and flowed, how unreliable mercurial forecasts could prove to be, and how devastatingly worrying a month-end was without sufficient monies to pay staff. He'd sailed close to the wind on more than one occasion, but he'd been chastened, survived and moved on.

Heady days.

What do you remember about your first few years in business? Do you look back and reminisce with fondness or wonder how you got away with it?

Breaking the spell

He wasn't certain when the magic stopped keeping pace with the expansion, but it had. He reflected that maybe there had only ever been three wishes available and he'd used up his in the early days, before he'd reached a staff of twenty and doubled his office space and willingly gifted a larger slice of himself to his bank. Maybe that was fanciful nonsense fuelled by his increasing sense of turbulence and sleep deprivation, but whatever had worked then didn't work now and that was fact.

In another beautiful irony, he now owned more data than he'd ever thought possible. More spreadsheets, more lines of code and more records than the shed could ever have ingested. But he also knew less.

Are you able to monitor the most important measures in your business?

The market he'd known intimately back in his shed days had accelerated and grown at an unprecedented pace. Many of his early competitors had sold up or been swallowed whole by others, creating businesses with significantly greater reach and buying power than he enjoyed. Start-ups appeared almost weekly, often with quirky names and alternative, colourful propositions. The launch and social media noise they made masquerading as brand-new offers frustrated him. Two of his larger clients had been swayed despite his best efforts to retain them, leaving him with a significant hole in his income and a rattled sales team.

Price had begun to trump value in the minds of many customers and he felt himself slowly drifting backwards as he found what he'd always known to be true no longer holding sway.

Do you ever think you'd be alright if it weren't for customers?

While he would always treasure the freedom his business afforded, the gnawing worry about cash and sales, salaries and people was exhausting and never-ending. Wanting to grow and change but uncertain where or how to; so not beginning at all became the default.

Do you find that figuring out what exactly to measure can stop you from taking any action at all?

There were moments when he envied the apparent security of his friends' jobs. Those that had applauded and perhaps envied his courage to quit corporate life were now enjoying multiple promotions, feather-lined benefits packages and cars that were miraculously replaced before their dashboards had an opportunity to celebrate the addition of a sixth zero to their mileage counts.

His, on the other hand, was well on its way to 160,000 and even the 'We'll buy anything that still has an engine' sites had stopped tempting him with offers. It was worth so little now that he doubted it could even be swapped for the new pair of super-lightweight bike wheels he'd been coveting. Dream on.

Does it sometimes feel like you're taking two steps forward and one step back?

The sales fairy

The beginning was innocuous enough. It'd been another long day when he parked up and walked into a brightly lit foyer full of brightly lit people offering hellos, business cards and slightly congealed finger food. He'd smiled as an image of 'speed dating for business dummies' flashed across his thoughts and then allowed himself to be shepherded into an anonymous hall full of chairs facing forward.

Ninety minutes later he was back in the foyer clutching a leaflet and musing about the apparent virtues of adopting a fully supported, 'proven to double your business', radically different sales approach that had delivered success 'Everywhere' (with a capital E). On the open market, and with a free sales tool thrown in for good measure, it was worth a king's ransom. Apparently. Magic wasn't explicitly mentioned in the presentation, but the claims made offered him some of what had walked out on him.

He held off being seduced for a long while. Maybe it was the supersonic jet graphics and the feeling that he might or should be able to do it for himself that kept him away, notwithstanding the fees that somehow managed to present themselves as being perfectly reasonable until compared to his weekly profit.

The approach offered whispered promises of success for a tiny and easy upfront commitment. Of course, there would be no guarantees, no shared risk, but wasn't life and business like that anyway? Other people had done it – so could he.

When times are tight, is it crazy to commit more funds to promises that might not be kept?

Some days he would have preferred to stay hidden in his shed. But doing this himself failed to recast his original spells and eventually he sent two of his staff on an open course. After hours of tunnelling through a plethora of web pages all offering the same thing packaged in differing shiny ways, he stuck a virtual pin in a virtual advert, clicked accept and dispatched them in hope to a real training venue.

They reported having had a great time. They chatted with the rest of his staff and extolled the virtues of the fairy cakes on offer during the breaks. They'd met some interesting people and learned some new ideas they claimed to be keen to try.

He put the moment down to nerves when they failed to agree on the structure they'd been practising for eight hours and when he asked them for more details about what they'd got from the £1,500 one-off day. Never mind, they were motivated, energised and ready to fly.

How do you get the best out of your team?

They returned to their desks, each clutching a file and a heavily branded pen, and for a while he was hopeful that this was where salvation lay. A new aura returned to the office that week, as did his optimism. Others in the team were catching the newly minted hints and tips by osmosis and they appeared synchronised and successful.

By the end of that same month the files lay untouched, and by the end of the next they had cast their own levitation spells and relocated themselves to the shelving at the back of the office.

Do you ever get the feeling your team don't always tell it exactly as it is?

Nothing was explicitly said. In a moment of uncertainty and distracted by an order that had gone astray, he'd missed (or in moments of self-flagellation, bottled) the opportunity to pursue why. He suspected his team had returned to a way of working that was already entrenched and easier to pursue (their inboxes, which by then had trebled in size). By dint of him not being around to focus minds, the new had been squashed by the current.

Everything had reset to normal again – not the old, buzzing normal but a, 'What the heck next?' normal.

He eventually mounted a rescue party for the learning in the hope it could be resuscitated. He retrieved the files from their place gathering dust alongside a dead monitor and two disembowelled headsets and turned the key elements into a guide to use during calls with clients. That idea outlived the original training course but two months on, other than the solitary line in his bank statement, few traces remained.

How many times have you spent money on developing your people only to watch the learning and energy wither and die?

A customer relationship management (CRM) system was next to arrive – sales magic via a blend of automated execution and rigorous process being the guaranteed recipe for growth and success. Yes, unscrambling and migrating his data had taken twice as long as the proposal he'd agreed to, and yes, things had got worse before they got better as his business grew used to the new ways of collecting and using the data. Osmosis was replaced by suspects and win ratios and a new language of certainty appeared almost overnight.

Maybe it should have been obvious to him that something wasn't quite translating. Maybe if he'd not been so busy taking the place of absent staff, chasing bad debt, following up deliveries and sorting out postage rates he'd have noticed sooner, but he didn't. By the time he did, the data within the system was being treated with such disdain by everyone around him that the entire system was no more than a repository for dashed dreams.

Are you reliant on systems that not everyone believes in?

His team took to blaming the agnostic system for its inadequacies and by inference, him for his purchase of it. No one trusted anything it reported and in turn he sensed that trust was a currency he was beginning to run short of.

Rather than focusing their minds on how the new CRM-based measures could improve customer service, the team's energy was spent mainly on debating whether the reports were right or wrong. Two of his team who'd been with him from the beginning left him for 'careers' that their positions with him could never replicate.

An unforeseen happy consequence of this had been the arrival of an apprentice with the makings of digital marketing skills. The CRM debate had pushed him to consider how his sales funnel actually worked and how his leads were generated. Thanks solely to his apprentice, his business now had an improved presence in the digital world.

He was able to expand his ecommerce platform and enhance its sophistication and ease of use – thanks in part to his apprentice's college coding and IT course. It cost him less to administer, cost less to achieve a sale and was providing increasing additional revenues for him.

What he was yet to fathom out was, 'What did this mean?' and how best to capitalise on it. What he did know was that he was now personally responsible for the management, the learning and the administration of the entire charabanc an apprentice materialises with.

He was certain that sustained growth was within reach and scale was a realistic goal, but the challenge of how and where to begin eluded him.

How do you identify your most important customers?

People who'd happily worked alongside each other for years and helped each other had begun to compete and bicker. Not all the time, but enough to worry him. Despite his best intent, introducing a commission scheme somehow made it worse.

Where previously his team had cheerfully co-operated and looked out for each other, he was now hearing second-hand how they artificially laid claim to clients they didn't own and blocked access to opportunities for others. It unnerved him and not knowing how to resolve this without alienating the team was making things worse.

Every article he read, every business book he scanned and every conversation he had all pointed him in different and often contradictory directions. Advocates of cultural change competed with process improvers. Peddlers of presenting skills did battle with mindset and resilience.

Are you clear on your critical sales measures?

Unable to make head or tail of this, he consoled himself by making an entirely different decision.

He supposed someone better qualified might have described it as an avoidance strategy for having to do some hard thinking about his business. He increased his AdWords spend, ensuring he appeared at the top of every search.

It was a spur-of-the-moment decision and gained him a puzzled frown from his marketing manager (who'd muttered something about having a plan) but it felt like an easy decision to make.

Do you know what's really important to your customers?

The team were briefly infected with the promise of success from new enquiries that his increased spend began to generate and his talk of good times to come and increased commissions kept them persevering.

He was aware of mutterings about tyre kickers, increased time-wasting and far more tiny orders being placed as a result of the new AdWords campaign, but he chose to ignore the moans. He wasn't at all certain which leads were good or how best to track them in the CRM but at least it was action.

One rainy afternoon, when he'd been avoiding a conversation with his courier about a damaged delivery a client was demanding a refund for, he did begin to ponder which part of his increased spend was the effective portion, but it fried his brain and left him none the wiser. So the spend had continued and he'd chosen the conversation with the courier instead.

How many people really contribute to sales success in your business?

With the benefit of hindsight, perhaps he should have predicted what this increased activity would mean elsewhere in his business. Sales did briefly increase but it soon became apparent that by only sprinkling magic across his sales team he had created chaos elsewhere.

Production scheduling and inventory control began to creak and groan and then in week nine almost toppled over. His team had the skills to respond to gentle fluctuations and the occasional last-minute customer demand. Now they were drowning in the sudden complexity and volume of increased orders, made worse by orders being recorded incorrectly in the sales team's haste to process them.

The effort to stabilise things almost cost him his sanity. It definitely cost him three nights' sleep and some fingernails.

How certain are you that changes you make in your business won't just relocate your problems and magnify them en route?

In an attempt to ensure orders were correct he insisted that he check every one, hunting for the errors or commitments that would fox production and risk his reputation. In the office or on his tablet at home, it became all-consuming and he sensed resentment building.

The adventure and potential he cherished was in danger of becoming a lead weight.

Advice from friends was enticing yet contradictory – all based upon their own experiences of a method, a solution or a book they'd read and none of which reflected where he found himself right now. None of which recognised how ensnared he felt.

He'd spent thousands of hours and thousands of pounds searching for improvements that had individually shown promise but somehow failed to aggregate into sustained growth. He wasn't just requesting a purchase order from procurement to fund another initiative – it was his money from his bottom line and burning it on further random help was not an option.

Who could he blame but himself?

Untangled

Everything within his business was totally inter-twined – he saw that now and he didn't know what to change for fear of making things much worse.

With the tendrils beginning to coil, he was Tangled and uncertain.

Do you recognise the maze? Do you feel Tangled?

We know sales can look complicated. You want help figuring out your most important customers and the right prices and discounts to charge them, but you want more than theoretical solutions from consultants. You want your sales team to be well-skilled and hungry, but you haven't got all week to supervise them. You want your whole business doing right by your customers without having to be prompted, but you can't (yet) afford an experienced sales manager.

Building a sustainable sales capability demands relentless focus and a willingness to adapt and amend all of your business activities to ensure they all connect appropriately and offer long-term scalable success and improvement – not just a fleeting moment of sales illusion delivered by hints and tricks. It transforms your activity from sales being what 'some of your business does some of the time' to 'what all of your business does all of the time', making sales a way of life.

This book will help you out of the maze. It will help to reboot your sales focus and energy and get you the customers you deserve. Not by peddling one-off quick fixes or listing hints and tips or focusing on one element of your sales process or skills to the exclusion of all else. You need something to enable you to make choices and act based upon an understanding of the complete interconnectedness of sales across the entirety of your business. You need to be Untangled.

PART ONE
SALES MYTHS

Introduction:
Sales Myths

Not many people are sales professionals. It might offer greater creativity, but it doesn't have the cachet of being an accountant. Nor will many years of successful sales results see you feted as a professional in the way a highly paid lawyer or a consultant surgeon might be.

In fact, if you're highly successful in sales you might well end up not selling at all. You'll more likely find yourself running a business or acting as a general manager. Many people will have held sales jobs – after school in Costa or a Saturday job in Mountain Warehouse – but for most people this is a stopping-off point. It's pocket money rather than a future they aspire to, hence the minimum wage.

Study sales professionally though, and you see that big companies get that sales is about building capability. That's why they have HR partners. Many directors in these organisations complain that their role is too much about process, procedure and politics. As sales director there's often limited space for creativity, and time spent on fixing customer problems diminishes, but working with those organisations you learn the rounded set of skills that help place customers at the heart of a business, making customers central to all operations, from marketing and finance through to supply.

Small businesses don't always have this grounding. In many cases the heads of these companies don't know there is such a thing as sales capability so it's not something they shop for. Too often, 'sales' is just a number and trying to grow it no more than a case of selecting the right tactics. Asking a friend or family member how to fix conversion rates or improve your CRM reports will elicit an answer to do no more than that. Unless they are sales professionals, they don't know any better either.

This problem is horribly amplified by Google. Google might be great for answering queries, but it can only answer the question you ask. If you're not a sales expert and start searching for solutions, all it can ever be is a mirror. You tell it what you don't know, and it tells you who can fix that specific problem. There might be much talk about Artificial Intelligence, but Google isn't yet able to unpick what you're thinking and feeling. Unless you ask how to build sales capability it won't tell you. All it will do is provide people who offer the service you've searched for and who'll charge you for it.

Why does this matter? Because big businesses already know this and build a sales capability accordingly. And you compete against them. You grudgingly recognise that their superior purchasing power means they'll receive more generous pricing than you. Give a supplier the same brief and their volume and scale will return a more competitive rate. But worse than this, because they are building a sales capability step by step, they are briefing suppliers more effectively and asking smarter questions than a small company. Not only do they achieve keener prices, but they've got a smarter shopping list.

Many of these larger corporates could easily pick through the list of sales myths in this section, identifying those with real validity and dismissing others, but smaller companies may hear these tales whispered and wonder whether some of them are true.

The problem with myths, of course, is when you start believing them. When it becomes difficult to separate fact from fiction, best practice begins to look tangled.

Ask yourself how many of these myths you've come across. If you have found yourself believing more than three or four of these in the course of running your business, then you're perilously close to entering the sales maze.

1
Sales Myth #1: Sales Is About Winners And Losers

Start here. Do not pass go. Wind back to something way more important than sales. Wind back to you. When it was just you – when you hadn't yet embarked on this madcap rollercoaster called 'running your own business'.

What made you gamble with the higher education your parents funded and abandon the security of a monthly paycheck? What made you sidestep the status of becoming a professional accountant, lawyer or whatever? Why did you make your choice?

Is it really a myth?

Received wisdom (aka what our gran said) lends its support towards this being a myth. Long-standing adages like, 'Treat others as you want them to treat you,' and, 'What goes around, comes around,' point to the centuries-old wisdom of collaborating with those around you.

The motor industry is an example where decades of collaboration have created 'just-in-time' supply chains, with partner organisations working together to improve efficiencies and reduce costs.

For some people, though, it's not a myth. These people are so highly focused on individual achievement and their own personal goals that nothing ever stands in the way of winning. Sales means money, prestige and getting one over on the losers. Such relentlessly competitive people might believe that winning is everything – second is nowhere.

Sir Philip Green, the head of the Arcadia Group, has attracted widespread criticism for his tax affairs and treatment of BHS workers' pensions. So hard-hitting is the criticism that he's been referred to as the 'unacceptable face of capitalism'.[1] Yes, you can be a millionaire running a business this way: the question

---

1   'Sir Philip Green: From "king of the High Street" to "unacceptable face of capitalism"', BBC News (27 November 2020), www.bbc. co.uk/news/business-36139828, accessed 14 January 2021

is whether you want to be. That's why this is about you. It's about your purpose – about the type of business you want to run and the type of person you wish to be.

Does the winner take it all?

If you want to create an organisation where everyone is squeezed for every last drop then your strategy is a simple one, but one that takes boundless energy because once you start squeezing the pips, it doesn't stop. Suppliers, customers, investors, staff – all are opportunities to strike a better deal. It can make you money and it will make you enemies for sure. We've witnessed organisations restructure operations in just this way. Staff are misled and contracts with suppliers broken. Anybody unhappy is backed into a choice of taking legal action or walking away empty-handed.

Does this work for the company? No. By wheedling their way out of contractual terms they certainly get away with non-payment of a few items that they really ought to honour. On the other hand, staff and suppliers leave at the first opportunity, taking all their industry expertise with them. Inevitably, over the next few months conversations throughout the sector spread the message that the acquiring company has a reputation for dirty tricks.

Does it matter?

It really is down to the sort of business you want to run. Take a simple example: is it OK for a sales person to trick their way past the managing director's PA to get an appointment?

> CALLER: Can I speak to the MD please?
>
> PA: May I ask who's speaking?
>
> CALLER: Yes, it's Jeff from SuperSelling Inc.
>
> PA: Is she expecting your call?
>
> CALLER: Yes, we spoke a few days ago.
>
> PA [shouting across the open-plan office to the MD]: Julie, do you know someone from Super-Selling Inc?
>
> MD: Never heard of them…
>
> PA: Sorry, she's in a meeting right now.

Is there anything really wrong with this conversation (apart from it not working this time)? Some people will think this is a quite clever sales trick and a quick Google search will show you're not alone.

The foreign currency exchange sector (FX) is awash with boutique businesses competing among themselves and with the banks for clients. Hordes of young people sit at desks charged with chasing the promise of jam (and a large shiny bonus) tomorrow by creating new leads today. They earn their stripes by cold-calling companies who are likely to have a need for this service – those who import or export goods or services as well as high-net worth individuals with cash to spend globally.

Getting past the gatekeeper (often an influence- and access-wielding PA) is the focus of their day and the cause of many rebuttals and much frustration. Some FX businesses have recognised that learning the names of PAs, taking time to develop these relationships, and genuinely engaging them in an honest conversation about why they're calling and what they're hoping to achieve delivers results. Yes, it takes longer and requires rapport and patience, but over time it results in better help and eventually access to the person they are hoping to speak with. Others persist in training tricks.

In the customer's shoes

If you're the PA to a finance director your entire day is likely to be one of constant interruptions via phone and email from hundreds of FX sales people all trying to get around, past or through you to the person you are there to protect and support.

If you're tricked once into doing this, wouldn't you be on the lookout next time that same voice or number appears on your phone? And what if your conversation progresses to the point of specifying a quote or even placing an order and then in what is now friendly conversation it transpires that the salesperson misled the PA in the first instance? What does that say about trust and your reliability? Be aware that over time you end up with the customers you deserve.

We strongly believe that it's possible to train customers. Like encouraging an overactive puppy, you might need a few attempts, but over time they figure out the way to get the best from you and adjust their behaviour accordingly. So, if you strike a deal with a customer that works for both of you, follow through on commitments and pay on time and you'll find that they'll reciprocate. Conversely, if you're prepared to sacrifice trust to land an order then you might win the deal this time, but you'll eventually end up in a state of permanent paranoia, always believing the other guy is out to get you.

2
Sales Myth #2: My Ten Biggest Customers Are My Most Important

Ask many business owners who their most important customers are, and the response is often a perplexed look followed by the words, 'My ten biggest.' The Pareto principle is a power law distribution theory which observes that most things have an unequal distribution. Commonly referred to as the 80/20 rule, in sales this applies to your customers in that 20% of them generally deliver 80% of your revenues.[2] Rank your customers from biggest to smallest and there is almost always a long tail of small ones with a lesser number being most important. Let's be serious: you almost certainly can't win by focusing on the smallest opportunities.

---

2   P Nair, 'What's the 80/20 rule in business? Are you doing it right?', *Real Business* (27 July 2020), https://realbusiness.co.uk/80-20-rule, accessed 14 January 2021

BEWARE THE LONG AND WAGGY TAIL

Interrogate[3] was a fast-growing IT business in Shoreditch that successfully dominated its industry niche. After years of informally treating some of its clients differently and somewhat randomly, they decided to instigate a formal categorisation of clients and apportion resource and investment accordingly. All clients were duly ranked based only on sales revenues, with account profitability and cost to serve not considered at this point. As with most businesses, the resulting Pareto curve identified the relatively small number of clients contributing the largest sums and these were duly appointed key accounts.

It was how the other end of the Pareto – the long and waggy tail – got treated that became a salutary tale in what happens when the wrong metrics or single perspectives are used to identify best and worst. Some 170 clients were bundled together as the tail and handed to a long-serving and long-suffering sales person. Lauren had already dealt with many of these clients and there were many others she had not come across before. Some had received no customer love for a number of years and had been directed to the support desk for help or to annoy on an ad hoc basis.

This was Lauren's 'golden opportunity' to re-establish contact, develop these clients and grow their spend (or at least put up their prices to market parity). If she could achieve increased sales targets of new products while she was there, that would be much appreciated – except

---

3   The case studies we give in this section are all based on real examples, but we've anonymised them. The companies and individuals we refer to are all fictitious.

that when she did visit them it transpired that they had no money and what they were already spending constituted everything they had. Nor did they want more innovation or faster upgrades. What they really loved was that they now had a person, a name and an email address to whom they could download all their issues, expecting instant resolution. They could demand regular face-to-face meetings to discuss these – after all, she was now *their* account manager, wasn't she?

That's when profitability and cost to serve entered stage left dressed as pantomime baddies waiting to spoil the story. It didn't take long for us to demonstrate that if Lauren stopped for a latte to top up her caffeine reserves as she drove to a client then the profitability in many of these clients was ruined.

When you're starting out in business (and we've been there) then every last customer is vital. Your first, second and third customers – and some that come a little while after – are essential in paying bills, keeping the lights on and funding the occasional well-deserved holiday. Plus, they are emotionally crucial in giving you that feeling that you are onto something meaningful; something that so obviously adds value to business owners.

But not all customers are created equal. Once you're beyond this first-date phase the reality is that some customers are more important than others. They all deserve a consistent level of courtesy, professionalism and customer service, but when it comes to tough decisions about how much marketing and promotion funding you spend with them – or how much of your costly sales team time they eat up – then size is not the only criteria.

It's not all about size

This has big implications for your team, because not all sales people are created equal. Sure, we've all seen those special relationships where one of the sales team strikes up a great relationship with a certain customer, or the customer that nobody really enjoys dealing with that somehow Jenny or James seems to have the knack of keeping cool. But that's about relationships.

It's not because your sales team have a diverse set of skills that enables them to achieve different outcomes from a range of customers. That's a sales capability on a whole different level. Some customer/sales relationships are easy to line up. The customer who needs lots of data can be paired with a sales person with great analysis skills; the customer with a proactive marketing team can be teamed up with one of your more creative employees.

But if you have a customer you want to spend less money with (and that's the only way you can spend more with the others) then a certain skill set is needed. It also requires a different mindset. If Lauren is great at controlling funds with lesser priority customers, then how do you keep her motivated knowing she might never manage your most glamorous customer? What impact does it have on your bonus structure when some customers aren't really invested for growth?

An unpredictable company reorganisation meant that, as a national account manager, Martin looked after one major grocery account for ten days. In his first – and final – meeting he agreed on a new way of running promotion multibuys with the buyer. It's what he had done with other customers and it seemed right for the business at the time. On unexpectedly handing back responsibility for the account, his predecessor said, 'For ten years I've been refusing multibuy funding and you gave it away in ten days.' Different sales person, different outcome.

The supplier doesn't matter

Let's step back a moment and think about this strategically. Why can't we just assume our ten largest customers are our most important and get on with the real job?

To begin with, it's worth thinking about how a smart business will look at its supplier base. Let's say you're running a buying organisation with fifty suppliers in one category. The sector doesn't matter. You could be buying beers for Wetherspoons with well over fifty breweries to choose from or you could be a housebuilder with fifty different manufacturers of roof tiles. The principles will be the same – you'll segment your suppliers along the lines in the diagram below:

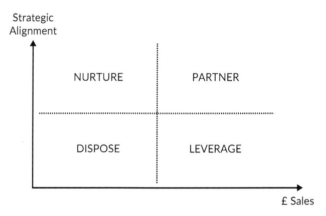

The bottom axis here is self-explanatory. You could replace sales with profit, but it's a simple way of denoting your largest suppliers as most important. The vertical axis allows more variation as 'strategic alignment' can be whatever you choose. It could simply be about generating investment so suppliers deemed to be a strong strategic fit are those willing to pay the most. It could be about innovation, with the buying organisation keen to find new ways of improving their own customer proposition. It might be about reliability, with consistent supply and quality the key determinant. It could be a combination of these and more.

What's critical to understand is that few suppliers make it into the partner box. For one thing the Pareto law applies in virtually all markets, with the majority of suppliers relatively small. Perhaps 80% of suppliers sit on the bottom half of this chart, which for most means either their customers are trying to dispose of them or at least prepared to beat them on price until they walk away. Of the remaining 20%, many won't be suitable partners because their innovation rate is slow, their supply chain is erratic, or maybe they simply don't want to sacrifice the margin needed to grow really close to the customer.

Something we often see, and in widely diverging industries, is how suppliers repeatedly overestimate how distinctive their product is and exaggerate their importance to the customer. Get wrapped up in an internal perspective of why your product or service is what the customer really needs and you'll find yourself in that bottom-right box: chasing revenue with a customer who sees your business as one to exploit and always being squeezed on price.

So how many of those fifty small breweries will be strategically important to the Wetherspoons buyer? How many are really irreplaceable? It's probably a handful, most likely fewer than five.

Take away from this diagram just one message: most suppliers don't really matter. Scale helps, but scale alone won't see you in that top five. If scale is your only strength, then growth will simply see you running ever faster, margins shrinking as you race to the bottom.

3
Sales Myth #3: We Can Absorb Cost Price Increases This Year

Not only is the potential prize of managing price significant, but the cost of doing nothing can be equally catastrophic. As you can see below, an average small business in the UK can be bankrupt in four years if they never find the right time to put through a price increase.

To begin with, this doesn't look like a tangle. The business could be performing well, staff turnover is low and customers are happy. The business is making a profit and has done for the last two or three years.

The volatility of relationship between price and margin is what makes this so sensitive. You can probably name friends or acquaintances who've encountered problems through absorbing cost increases and here is an example that came to mind for us. The organisation had started down this road with well-intended decisions in year one. One year ran into multiple years until the situation was acute and we were called in to help untangle the net profit problem.

DON'T DELAY A PRICE INCREASE

Newepharm was a global pharmaceutical company, who for one reason or another (and another) hadn't taken a price increase in the UK for seven years. Exchange rates had now shifted and they wanted to remedy some of this shortfall. A double-digit price increase was budgeted.

The problem, of course, was that their customers were having none of it. Newepharm could painfully count back each of the seven years, with a spreadsheet to support the detail. The customers – most likely on their seventh buyer in the same period – couldn't care less.

The situation was worsened by the fact the retailers had nudged up prices in the intervening seven years and were selling above recommended price. They had implemented a price increase anyway and banked it in the form of enhanced margin. For the retailer this was a year one scenario – today's price was what they expected and anything upwards was undesirable.

In the end we were able to help the supplier gain an increase some 4% ahead of inflation. A good result in any circumstances, but scant consolation for the lost years.

How can an inability to take a price increase have such a dramatic impact on profitability? It's the sensitivity of pricing. The beauty of price is that every *extra* penny on price drops straight to the bottom line. But the reverse also holds true. Absorbing cost price changes is the fast track to oblivion.

From boom to bust

ACMA is a manufacturing company that turns over £1m. Obviously it's not a large American Company that Makes Everything, it's too small for that, but it makes Allsorts.

The cost of manufacturing, including raw materials is £500k, so gross profit is £500k. Other costs come to a total of £400k, which includes £180k for staff costs, £80k for rent and rates, and £60k for utilities. Net profit is a healthy £100k, or 10%.

£000	Current
Sales Turnover	1,000
– Cost of Goods	500
= Gross Profit	500
– Staff Cost/Wages	180
– Rents and Rates	80
– Utilities/Fuel	60
– Other	80
= Net Profit	£100
%	10%

The market is challenging, with minimum wage nudging up labour costs, utilities charging extra for smart meters and exchange rates against the dollar edging downwards. Overall input costs in year one increase by about 3%. Customers are squealing about this, so ACMA decides not to ask for a price increase this year.

The next year it's more difficult to ask. Yes, costs have risen by another 3%, but the new buyer has said she needs time to understand her new job and can't agree to price increases during that time.

By year three continuing inflation means ACMA could do with a price increase, but they want 6% to claw back last year and nobody will agree to that. Plus, their nearest competitor has invested in new machinery and they've heard they are offering discounts to key customers. Rather than put up prices and compete against these promotion discounts, ACMA decide to hold cost prices for one more year. This works to some extent, and they manage to hold sales steady in a tough market. Sales will get a bonus. Hurrah.

Except the accountant isn't happy. Yes, sales are still £1m, but cost of materials is now £546k (+3% over three years). Staff costs have risen to £197k and other costs are also up. Net profit is just £17k and the MD asks how, when the business was perfectly healthy just three years earlier, they could now go bust by May?

| £000 | Current | 3 Yrs No Price Increase | |
		Inflation Rate	£
Sales Turnover	1,000	0%	1,000
– Cost of Goods	500	3%	546
= Gross Profit	500		454
– Staff Cost/Wages	180	3%	197
– Rents and Rates	80	3%	87
– Utilities/Fuel	60	3%	66
– Other	80	3%	87
= Net Profit	100		17
%	10%		2%

4
Sales Myth #4: We Can Recoup Today's Discount On The Next Deal

Price is such a critical factor in the success of a business that it bears a second look. Achieving list price isn't easy, but it's a simple concept to grasp. This chapter is about the hidden dangers in price discounting – harder to spot, but potentially equally damaging.

Each of the approaches you'll read about here sound perfectly reasonable and in the right circumstances something you'd call good business, but any one of the three can present a painful problem for your business if you're not aware of why you're doing it and how often.

Marginal cost

Price is typically established by taking your list price and deducting discounts that either your customers demand or your sales people offer. Then you take off the cost of production to give gross margin. Behind this of course is the overhead of running the business, so the overall net profit might be, say, 10%.

Imagine you're running a signage business that's been growing well. Your production is outsourced, which gave you real agility when you started, but lately you've come to realise that some orders are taking too long to turn around. Worse, the occasional order has been returned by customers unhappy with product quality.

Confident in the prospects for expansion, you buy a shiny new large-format printer which is parked in what used to be your loading bay. The accountant is letting you depreciate it over five years and tells you that not only will quality improve, but your gross margin will improve by some ten percentage points. Happy days.

You've hired a graphic designer to ensure the equipment is used to its full potential and for the first couple of months you revel in the quality and speed with which you fulfil orders. No more delays. No more printing errors.

Then a large regional business gets in touch via your website. Previously you'd have struggled to match their volume needs, but with your new printer fully operational you can put in a couple of evenings and the job will be complete. You've noticed that the flatbed is fantastic when it's needed, but much of the time it's sitting idle – as is the designer, who you've spotted is as interested in designing their Instagram posts as they are your artwork. This big order is way below your normal cost price, but you decide to take the volume. After all, you're already paying for the printer and operator, so the only additional cost is the card needed for the job itself.

It's good business, right? Well… It might be.

If the alternative really is for equipment and people to sit idle then there is obviously a financial benefit in having them produce something for you and generate some revenue, but there is risk inherent in this. It's easy to get seduced into doing more business at marginal cost. Before you know it, your sales team are happy to offer the discounted rate (which helps them hit their volume bonus) and worse, your customers have come to expect it. Not just the attractive large customer who came with the prospect of really driving your top line, but others who you have spent years educating about how your proposition delivers value, not price.

So, don't dismiss this option, but be disciplined about where and when you allow it and what it means for your price and range going forward.

Customer cross-subsidy

For most businesses pricing policy is like the Highway Code: it's a function of a long and complicated history and is of little practical help in getting you where you want to be.

Why do some big customers pay more than others? It's just evolved that way. In effect, one customer is cross-subsidising another by paying a little more for your product or service. Look closely and those with the best deal are usually the most aggressive. Unfortunately, unless you have a defensible price list and a tough sales team, those buyers who shout, bang the table and threaten you with de-lists tend to be the ones who get the best deal. In rapidly evolving markets this is a dangerous place to be.

Even before the impact of coronavirus, the UK retail market has come under huge pressure in recent years. Store closures, increasing rents and rates, and increases in minimum wage have created the perfect storm of flat sales and rising costs. This has resulted in a relentless wave of mergers and acquisitions across the high street, with Argos bought by Sainsbury's, Boots merging with Walgreens in the

US, and Tesco snapping up Booker's cash and carry business.

All of these deals carried price implications for suppliers. Accepted practice for the advisors on these deals is to compare price files across the two retailers – it's part of the due diligence process. Then they build into their forecasts the price improvements to be gained by assuming future purchases will be made at the lowest of the two prices. The supplier pays.

In 2018 Sainsburys and Asda announced a mega-merger. The Sainsbury's leadership team set out projected 'savings' of £500m that they explicitly stated would come from suppliers: an end to the cross-subsidy. Cue howls of anguish from beleaguered suppliers and – to cut a long story short – a deal that was eventually scuppered by the Competition and Markets Authority.[4]

Suppliers got away with it this time, but the clear lesson from this saga is to do everything in your power to keep pricing consistent and equitable across your customer base. You never know when the next big deal is coming and your customers will always – *always* – see their suppliers as part of the funding.

---

4   J Armour, 'Sainsbury's/Asda merger blocked: Analyst reactions', *The Grocer* (25 April 2019), www.thegrocer.co.uk/sainsburys-asda-merger/sainsburys/asda-merger-blocked-analyst-reactions-/592706. article, accessed 14 January 2021

BEWARE THE LURE OF DISCOUNT

We came across a variation of this cross-subsidy problem with Interrogate. They put much effort into creating price lists and discount structures that reflected a client's scale of purchase based upon prescribed criteria. In an incestuous sector where buyers appeared to be on continuous rotation between clients this was invaluable and defensible.

The pricing structure was smart enough to differentiate between one-off implementation fees and ongoing support. If we ignored the odd instance of enhancing a proposal by deliberately under-forecasting project duration it was an approach that served them well, except that they allowed themselves to be seduced by the promise of leveraged reputation.

A group of academic colleges insisted that their global reputation was so great that referencing Interrogate's systems would significantly enhance their sales line when other colleges flocked to copy them. Of course, this offer of largesse would only be forthcoming if matched by a reciprocating price, but never mind, the reputation they had would draw in other clients...

It didn't work out like that. The colleges were nervous about becoming reference sites for Interrogate in a market where product demonstrations and ease of use were key to converting prospective new clients. Worse, while the colleges' reputation for academic excellence were irrefutable, their reputation for being successful early adopters of new solutions was much less convincing. Their peers weren't persuaded and the march to Interrogate's door didn't materialise.

What eventually did appear were past employees of those colleges now happily installed elsewhere requesting a price reduction on behalf of their new employers.

Price unbundling

Supermarket wagons are such a familiar sight on the UK's roads that we rarely give a thought to what's in them or where they are going (unless you're stuck behind one in teeming rain, in which case you can be certain it's going where you are, only slower). There's a massive industry in ensuring these lorries are filled for as much of their journey time as possible. A major supermarket needs numerous deliveries each day to keep the shelves stocked, yet nothing goes back in the opposite direction.

Smart logistics systems have worked out a network of collaborating businesses local to each store that need transport in the opposite direction. Say a Tesco lorry is driven from Rugby to the store in Telford. A deal is done with a producer in Telford who needs transport back along the M6 and is happy to pay a discounted rate to fill Tesco's empty lorry. It's good for costs and it's good for the environment. It's good for Tesco, but it might not be ideal for you.

If, as a supplier, you had negotiated a price for your transport contract based on your predicted volume for the year, this Tesco arrangement will leave you with less volume. As the biggest UK grocer Tesco might represent a quarter of your business, so your negotiating power with suppliers has shifted overnight. It's cross-subsidy again. Your price for other customers must rise.

Price unbundling is, of course, something that has transformed the airline industry. In this case, it's new entrants like Ryanair and Easyjet that have unbundled pricing in an industry once dominated by national airlines such as BA, Air France and Alitalia. Stripping out costs once considered an essential part of flying has enabled these low-cost airlines to take a significant share of flight traffic across much of Europe, putting downward cost pressure on the established airlines.[5]

The thing with these three discounting bear pits is that they are not obvious like list pricing or promotions and this makes them especially dangerous. They can have an acute impact on a company's cash position because the net effect is giving away too much discount. Like any good traps they are obvious once you've discovered them but it's little consolation by then and you're left questioning how you could have been so naive as to not have spotted them in the first place.

5   E Picardo, 'An economic analysis of the low-cost airline industry', Investopedia (7 October 2020), www.investopedia.com/articles/investing/022916/economic-analysis-lowcost-airline-industry-luvdal.asp, accessed 14 January 2021

5
Sales Myth #5: My Sales Team Will Give Me Honest Feedback If Something's Going Wrong

One of the hardest things in management is telling your boss that they are wrong. Anybody spending just a few years in the corporate world will have experienced a boss who by common agreement isn't good. Maybe some of us – in the wrong place at the wrong time – have been that boss. Others will have found that this was the experience that acted as the trigger that propelled them towards leaving the corporate world and starting their own business.

Can I have a word?

In many of these situations that, 'Boss, can I have a word…' conversation won't have happened. It won't have happened because we might upset their feelings and because we're British and don't like to complain, but more than anything it won't have happened because the odds are stacked against us. Complain against the boss and by implication you're challenging the system – the same system that decides your annual pay rise, your rating in your annual review and your future career progression. It's easier and more predictable to suck it up and eventually move elsewhere.

It's a national fascination for us to watch how this plays out in professional sport. In today's Premier League, footballers – often paid more than their managers – have a certain amount of player power and there are cases where a manager is deemed to have 'lost the dressing room'. For all the foibles shown by the global millionaires who run today's football games, teams never seem to fall out with their club owners – all these cases are of teams falling out with their managers. Their argument isn't with Abramovich, Glazer or the Qatari wealth fund, but with the team manager.

Take this premise and then consider how likely someone is to take issue with the performance of a company owner. Not just your line manager, but the boss and the majority shareholder. It can only end one way and it won't be roses and chocolate.

BEWARE THE ECHO CHAMBER

Johan's story shows just how far things can go wrong when your team members don't speak up. Johan was an athletic, rugby-playing, 6-foot 4-inch company owner with a shock of blonde hair and a big personality. Over a twenty-year period he'd grown his health business from the ground up to attain a multimillion-pound valuation.

Johan loved a bit of showmanship and noise. Why sidle up to someone if you can shout across the office or sound a klaxon every time a new sale is made? He thought nothing of taking gaggles of his business out for drinks and participated loudly and with hearty exaggeration in the re-telling of tall tales. This attracted a certain crowd from his business. Others gave him a wider berth.

Johan was immensely successful and justified in believing his ways of working underpinned that. Except what used to be best practice had moved on. Markets changed, employee expectations evolved and his industry became much more heavily regulated.

At work Johan talked a lot about learning and the power of feedback: his feedback to others, on occasions delivered bluntly and subjectively and with an emphasis on personal failure. He was never quite so receptive to receiving feedback himself – about his own impact or his business. His defensive response quickly highlighted to everyone that feedback was awkward and maybe even damaging to your job prospects, all of which contributed to his sales manager choosing not to tell him that the ratios and conversion statistics he was extracting from their CRM tool were hugely inflated. The sales funnel on which he was basing his decisions was a dry well. Neither did his sales manager tell him that his interactions with new staff members left them demotivated and unnerved. The sales team was falling apart and his best talent leaving.

After spending decades building his business, Johan ended up in front of his industry regulator. The regulator wanted to know why unlicensed sales had been permitted and demanded that the business open to an external audit. The value of Johan's business halved within a matter of days, slashing investors' equity. Half the workforce were forced out in two messy months to balance the books. Nobody profited from this and there's no happy ending. It was simply horrible.

As this shows, the problem with not nurturing employee feedback is that it creates an echo chamber for company owners. In some businesses they can point to strong staff retention as a measure of good management, but in reality, it means anyone and everyone who's left behind agrees with the captain. The staff members who don't see eye to eye with the owner move on (usually at high speed) and those that are left don't have the desire or wisdom to challenge the boss. It's a workplace version of Stockholm Syndrome[6] where employees are kidnapped by their own inertia. As the owner you're left with a team that has a genetic weakness: they all agree with you.

---

6   L Lambert, 'Stockholm syndrome' (Brittanica, no date), www. britannica.com/science/Stockholm-syndrome, accessed 23 November 2020

Giving voice to employees

In the corporate world there's a concept called 'employee voice' where employees are encouraged to put forward their views on how the business can be better run. Sceptics will suggest this is another initiative which will help to fuel the HR engine for another few years, yet we repeatedly see that employees too often will not speak up even when they believe their boss is wrong.

To be clear, this is not about whistleblowing policies where people are encouraged to express concerns about potential rule breaches and financial misconduct. Those can and should continue to exist, but typically act as confidential reporting mechanisms to ensure business compliance. It's not about discipline, it's about engaging people in the business to give their best and feel that their contribution is valued.

There's a degree of objectivity built into these processes in big business, not least because both manager and employee can roll their eyes knowingly about another glossy brochure appearing from the HR team, but it presents a different – more personal – challenge in small companies.

These businesses are often led by an owner who knows intimately how and why everything in the organisation happens and they are best placed to answer questions and fix problems. The disadvantage with this, of course, is that no solution will ever surface which is better than the one the founder came up with. In truth, as the owner gets busier and finds more demands on their time, they can well become a bottleneck in decision processes rather than the productive go-to person they once were.

Getting to the bottom of what employees really think about the business and how they believe their contribution can be most valuable is something that needs a conscious effort. Of course, some business owners are natural collaborators and instinctively seek out the views and opinions of their teams but there are many more – and we've worked with a good number – who find it difficult to see beyond their role as the boss. It takes a bold step to acknowledge that the business can be stronger if it's not you at the head of everything.

There are plenty of ways of encapsulating this concept as a strategic challenge, for example, attracting and retaining the best people, creating a proactive company culture, or posing it as idea generation, but all need a determined and clear planning step to make this something your business is really going to set out to achieve.

At its heart this is an approach designed to encourage your team to give their best. To feel that they can speak up when they don't quite believe in what you're passionate about and to ask the stupid questions without worrying that doing so might prove to be a career-limiting step.

Time and again we've been invited into businesses with a clear instruction to 'fix' either a broken process or a broken person. Time and again we discover that it's the owner or owners who are setting the tone. Their staff are too fearful to tell them the truth and trust has disintegrated.

One client had gone to the effort of using a well-known tool to assess their senior leadership team dynamic to establish how well they operated, except no one trusted the owners to respond in an open-minded and consistent way. Every score given in the final published report reassured the owners that they were indeed a highly functional team. The behaviours and private conversations people were having with us suggested nothing of the sort. They were only too able to explain the cracks that were appearing and the relationships that were unravelling.

Imagine how it feels to uncover that your key staff choose not to challenge you and are scared to act on their own initiative as they don't trust your responses? Worse, imagine how it then feels to be faced with the realisation that as joint owners you don't even trust each other enough to speak up when one of you is out of line or hurting – that those around you knew this, but you hadn't had the courage to face it.

Be the change

What *you do* is vitally important here. In so many cases this will need the company owner to behave somewhat differently. You'll have to persist through the raised eyebrows and banter about whether you've been chatting to your business coach again, because sooner or later you'll be put to the test. Something will go wrong when it's least convenient for you: on a Monday when you're piled high with emails and the production plant grinds to a halt, or on a Friday when you've promised to treat your other half with an early finish and a nice dinner because you're not 'wedded to the business'.

You'll be under pressure to find a fix to a problem and one of the team will interrupt you with some half-arsed suggestion that you know you tried three years ago. Didn't work then and won't work now. Except… Was it a bad idea then or did it just not have the commitment that was needed to make it fly? What if the market has moved on and you've not quite tracked it? In that moment, your team will know whether there's any life left in this notion you mentioned a couple of months ago about people feeling free to speak up with ideas and there not being any such thing as a bad suggestion.

Call it right and next time one of your team might just prevent you running full pelt past the road sign marked 'Great Cockup'. Call it wrong and you'll be subject to the humiliation that comes with viewing a journey through the rear-view mirror. Everyone around you will look back on your ill-informed decision and say, 'I told you so.'

In business we often make decisions on topics we don't really know the answer to. It's part of the thrill. We all thought Brexit was taking a step into the unknown until coronavirus came along and showed us what hurtling into a void really looked and felt like.

In some cases, there's no road map – we can only choose a course based on the best knowledge available at the time. You may have a great track record of inventing products or services that disrupt a market or create completely new ones. If you have an impressive academic backstory and are proud of your ability to think or learn it can be seductive to assume that you have the answers for every element of your business and that no one else can think or act or create to the same standards as you, but do this at your peril. Your team may decide that you're arrogant and stop offering, and you risk finding out the hard way that they were right.

6
Sales Myth #6: I Need A Hungry Sales Team

One of the more unusual things we hear said about sales – and it's a frequently used descriptor – is when someone demands that their sales team is hungry. It's a cliché that's crying out for deeper and more specific thinking. A hungry dog might make an effective deterrent, but if it's fed on scraps it'll likely turn out aggressive and try to eat anything that's thrown its way – not what you want from a sales team.

Thinking smarter

It's no longer enough for headless sales teams to be chasing around the country. Businesses are only too aware of the increasing costs of having sales people on the road, with the cost of cars, fuel and sales bonuses adding to the equation. Targeting the right customers and focusing sales resources carefully is the new normal. Busyness is not good business.

It can be difficult for some business owners to grasp the contradiction between a 'hungry' sales team and the 'safety first, yes Boss' culture you read about in the last chapter. We worked with a company that stepped up its innovation cycle from creating one new product a year to delivering six. It was a fantastic effort from the marketing team, but one that sales would struggle to deliver with customers. The sales team knew this, but nobody felt able to raise their concerns during the initial planning sessions.

Bosses that demand a 'hungry' sales team don't like to hear reasons why things can't be done. This can become an irrational deafness that prevents them from hearing about legitimate business obstacles. If you're tempted to use the word 'hungry', then pause and ask yourself exactly what you mean. Do you want a professional sales team? An enthusiastic, motivated one?

We're all in it together

The second oddity about demanding a 'hungry' sales team is the fact that it is perceived as only attributable to sales. What do we mean by 'hungry'? If we mean 'enthusiastic', 'motivated' or 'proactive', wouldn't we want your teams to know that? We want people in marketing or finance to be proactive and show initiative – why do we only expect sales people to be 'hungry'?

Maybe the idea of the hungry sales team is more of an emotional concept. Every company needs a heartbeat – the why that gets everyone out of bed in the morning and helps create the long-term success of the business. Maybe it's the outgoing nature of sales people that creates the buzz, the energy and the optimism that keeps that pulse rate high, yet what's referred to as 'sales culture' rarely stops at the door of the sales team – it's a mindset and behaviour that's evident throughout the business: from production and order processing through to invoicing and credit control, everyone has an impact on how the customer experiences the business. Everyone impacts the next sale in their own small way.

SELF-SABOTAGE

Take our experience with the devices division of Newepharm. Their entire focus was selling life-saving capital goods to national healthcare systems. The whole team had seriously impressive scientific qualifications and experience – many to rival the people to whom they were selling. They knew their stuff.

The sales cycle was often long, complicated and buying decisions increasingly controlled by procurement teams. Months could be spent engaging the key users, demonstrating equipment, providing technical specifications and reports to substantiate claims. Visits to other sites already using the equipment would be arranged at significant costs, only to watch a change of senior staff bring a change of allegiance to another manufacturer and entirely scupper twelve months' effort in a heartbeat.

Often though, the competition for this dedicated sales team was much closer to home and more pernicious. Their own team of service engineers spent hours on their backs lying underneath machines, repairing parts and saving waiting lists from certain cancellation. We uncovered occasions when, over the obligatory post-job cuppa, the engineers were telling the hospital staff that the equipment they'd been sold was the wrong choice. Their equipment was market-leading, but in complex markets like this every purchase is a compromise – you don't extoll the benefits of the competition. How to starve your hungry sales team...

Customer first

It's clear that sales culture, hungry or not, is about people and how they behave. Customers rarely respect your job descriptions or functional boundaries – they just want what they need quickly, reliably and at a reasonable price. These customers are the ultimate arbiters of whether or not you have a sales culture, so this is as much about your internal business relationships as it is about how your sales team handles customers.

The risk in keeping your sales team 'hungry' is that they pursue customers too hard. From an internal perspective it might be exciting to see sales people banging gongs and sounding klaxons when deals come in, but the customer could be quite put-off by over-enthusiastic sales people. One organisation's 'hungry' sales person can easily be another's pushy sales rep.

A sales culture is a difficult thing to pin down as it's not something likely to appear as a key plank of a company's strategy. It's a behaviour and mindset that permeates every other priority but rarely something that stands alone. What is critical is that it's something that comes from the top. Nothing is more guaranteed to put a hungry sales team on a crash diet than believing that the boss isn't committed to customers in the same way they are.

So, continue to demand a positive sales culture, but do at least listen to the pragmatists in the sales team who might just be warning of legitimate barriers to growth.

LOST THEIR APPETITE

Medivent had a rollercoaster sales culture. On the one hand there was a real energy about sales performance, with a strong focus on the number of customers contacted each week. Strangely, though, in many respects the company had a truly lacklustre culture.

With insufficient emphasis on business outcomes people worked fixed hours and left for the day. Innovative ideas were quashed before being tested. Perhaps the saddest aspect of the culture was that nobody really gave their best.

The stakeholders in the business were weary. Tired of trying over and again to kick-start the machine and tired of worrying about their investment. Willing to sell but struggling to obtain their aspirational valuation. Fearing more of the same and feeling helpless to resolve it.

In this organisation you can see the relevance of the biological meaning of culture. Trapped in this ownership tangle, the founders had killed off the bubbling culture that had launched them from zero to hero in the early days and as they had lost their appetite, so had the team.

7

Sales Myth #7: You Can Kick A Sales Person And They Will Bounce Back Immediately

Sales people need to be able to take knocks. They need to be able to respond positively to calls that might be neither reasonable nor fair and to handle unreasonable or irrational customer objections, but that doesn't make them superhuman.

When we were students in the 80s the government hadn't yet come up with its recommendations for limiting weekly alcohol consumption to a certain number of units. Suffice to say had the targets been in place they would have undoubtedly been broken – often in a single night – so it's no surprise that Martin's first job was with a brewery. The company culture was a traditional, hierarchical structure. Managers were addressed as 'Mister' (we assume that ladies would have been called 'Mrs' but as there weren't any senior female personnel he never got to find out).

Long-standing brewing practices were reinforced through a unionised environment that meant people policies and procedures were adhered to. Sales performance was brutally judged. If you fell short of target with any sort of regularity you were issued with a verbal warning, which in due course could evolve into a serious disciplinary process. Considering this was the era of Guns N' Roses and *Neighbours*, it seems like another world, yet there are still businesses today that operate this 'hire and fire' approach to sales people. Get bums on seats, set a stretch target and see who makes it. The rest are dispensable.

NAMING AND SHAMING

Sunnybond Property operated like this until recently. If your role and your success at work become inextricably linked to your identity and worth as a human being, imagine what happens when your sales dry up. Place that within a culture that's not renowned for its sympathetic response to requests for help, coupled with an ability to demote any 'hero to a zero' in a nanosecond and people get hurt.

Missed outbound call rates, an inability to convert leads, missing sales revenues or just being deemed to be lacking in some indefinable 'va-va-voom' meant sales people were regularly reprimanded for their performance. Loudly, across the office and in front of their peers. Incentives that welcomed the winner to all-inclusive weekends of sun, sea or skiing also named and shamed the lowest performers with scorn, personal attacks and humiliation.

Staff turnover was over 30%. Fees to recruiters were astronomical and morale was low.

The wasted opportunity here was that raw talent wasn't nurtured. New starters didn't know the basics of selling, how to ask open questions, how to qualify a lead, or how to listen and how to plan their activity based upon their sales funnel and conversion rates. The result? The raw talent just walked away.

We're the last people to advocate clinging onto business relationships that aren't working, but most of us at least want to know we gave it our best. If you were ever to end up in front of an employee tribunal, they would insist on that as a minimum too.

Sales people will also typically be outgoing people who are happy to meet with others, explore their worlds and build relationships. Superficially at least, this makes them appear confident and sure of themselves, able to deal with tricky customers and come back smiling – but appearances can be deceptive. We know from the world of showbusiness that the most gregarious people are not always the most resilient. On stage they appear talented, funny and confident, but that's the act. Behind the scenes things can be different. The same applies to certain sales people. Handling awkward customers, dealing with the false promises about big orders next month and smiling when you're told you'll be paid on Friday. That's easy, it's the job. We've never met a sales person who enjoyed failure, but we've seen plenty who didn't make it. The gap? Recruiting the wrong people; lack of robust onboarding; unclear roles and responsibilities; conflicting targets and 'sales prevention' departments. None of them the responsibility of sales people. All of them a reflection of strategy and leadership.

Getting the right person in the right job is crucial here. As you will learn in the chapter on hunters versus farmers, some people will find too many negative responses dispiriting whereas others will simply be more fired up for the next call.

Under pressure

The question of increasing pressure on sales is clearly a highly nuanced discussion and we recommend being clear on the root causes of under-performance before any action is taken.

Deep down, not all sales people respond positively to pressure. That somewhat macho culture shouldn't lead you to believe that everyone is resilient underneath. Some really do need an arm round the shoulders or someone to look out for them. It might be how they handle the pressure of work. It might be about things going on in their lives that we've never asked about or they'll never share. But before you crank up pressure you need to know it's the right tool for the job. Getting it wrong can produce bad results indeed.

In an increasingly litigious business world, it can be painfully costly in unproductive wages and likely more costly in impact if one of your team takes months out of work with stress; but that is nothing compared to the emotional cost and guilt of knowing you've impacted someone's family stability or contributed to their mental health challenges. So listen – really listen. It might not be what you want to hear, but the root of that under-performance might be strategy or leadership and not about the sales team at all. You've been warned.

8
Sales Myth #8: With Sales You Get What You Measure

Half Man Half Biscuit – like the name of the famous indie band, this myth is about 50% true and 50% untrue.

For the sake of simplicity, we'd like to declare it entirely fact or fiction, but in practice there are two competing behavioural factors here. Firstly, sales people – especially those with bonus targets – will ensure they focus on key measures. It's in their blood. On the other hand, one of the inescapable principles of business is 'the law of unintended consequences'[7]

7   T Pettinger, 'Law of unintended consequences' [blog post], Economics Help.org (27 September 2019), www.economicshelp.org/blog/2381/economics/law-of-unintended-consequences, accessed 12 November 2020

which basically means that you sometimes end up with the opposite of what you hoped for.

It's scant consolation to note that politicians seem to suffer from this principle even more frequently than managers. In recent years, and with house prices rising beyond the means of many young adults, the government has invested much money (and PR) into the 'help to buy' scheme. The aim was to make it easier for first-time buyers to get a foot on the housing ladder. What actually happened (as reported by the Audit Office)[8] is that people who could already afford to purchase a house found it easier than before, while many of those who couldn't were still unable to. Meanwhile, private builders have enjoyed a subsidy-fuelled boom, with directors enjoying multimillion-pound bonuses. The law of unintended consequences.

Time for action

Sales team metrics and key performance indicators (KPIs) are frequently front of mind when someone talks about increasing pressure on a sales team. If we just get closer to the numbers then results will surely improve…

---

8   'Help to Buy: Equity loan scheme progress review' (NAO, 13 June 2019), www.nao.org.uk/press-release/help-to-buy-equity-loan-scheme-progress-review, accessed 14 January 2021

One of the challenges with this approach is the relationship between activity and outcome. Many sales teams are governed by assessment of what they do rather than what they achieve. Is a rep who completes the expected eight calls a day better than one who does six? Is a customer service operator who consistently overruns the average five minutes a call doing a worse job than their more punctual colleague?

The answer lies in what they *achieve*, not what they do.

We worked with a client who insisted his team needed to improve their lead conversion rates. If they all performed at the level of the best he explained as he waved a report at us, the business would improve by 40%. Except when we dug deeper, we found there was no real correlation between the conversion percentage rates and high sales numbers. Some of the team evidently weren't great at turning leads into new business, but they could identify the big opportunities and get them over the line, generating more revenue than some of their busier colleagues.

And it's not just sales. The MD of a business we worked with some years ago insisted that the whole team be at their desks during the working hours of 9am to 5.30pm. Other than for sickness, absence from the desk met with an interrogation about where you were and how that benefitted the business. The outcome? When it wasn't busy, people surreptitiously wrote a couple of private emails or browsed the web. When it was busy, they went home at 5.30pm regardless – that's what they were paid for.

Another client employed a small team of lead generation sales people who were tasked with and rewarded on gaining agreement from prospective clients to receive a company brochure and complete an initial questionnaire – all input measures. Their efforts were highly rewarded as they were right at the top of what could be a lucrative sales funnel. They were lauded as being best practice for other teams in the business to emulate. Except over time, conversions withered. What became apparent when we examined the data and listened to the calls being made was that no measure of quality and no qualification of potential (both outputs) were being made prior to seeking agreement to send a brochure. Brochures were being sent to anyone and everyone, so brochure targets continued to be hit and sales conversions continued to be missed. Be careful what you measure.

Setting sales targets

One of the toughest challenges in setting sales targets is avoiding the law of unintended consequences. It's what pops up when your targets aren't quite aligned with what you really want your business to be like. You also need to be careful of the data sets that you choose to use as measurement.

NAVIGATING UNKNOWNS

In Promlast, individual targets meant sales people ringfenced big customers from the rest of the team. They were too busy to properly develop new opportunities with these customers, but keeping them away from colleagues meant that they could rely on the annual top-up order being theirs. The company lost out.

A regularly repeated statement within Promlast had achieved almost mythical standing: 'We always win one in three.' It became a clarion cry and somewhat self-congratulatory, but on examining the publicly available industry sales data this appeared to be overstated. The value of revenue within Promlast was a long way below a third of the size of business being awarded across the sectors in which they competed.

Upon further digging it became apparent that the actual statistic was, 'We win one in three bids *that we know about.*' The sales team were successful in how they proposed and specified new proposals for business they were aware of, yet the business as a whole was losing share because of its inability to identify all potential opportunities within its space. The sales activity and measures changed soon afterwards.

Individual sales targets can be motivational for some people and, with the right customer portfolio, might put a rocket under the sales of your business, but if you're hoping for teamwork, they are more likely to place a bomb under it.

The impact we often see this having on business owners is their frustration that 'nobody cares as much as me'. Too right. You employ them so they won't care as much as you. For sure, employees care about their jobs and the good ones will care about the broader business and their team too, but the adrenaline that wakes you up before the alarm is largely the preserve of the owner.

Some of the most frustrated owners we meet are those with the most KPIs. Over-emphasising metrics, they've lost emotional connection with their teams and are left with the sense that they alone are carrying the can. Over time more measures, each with increased levels of apparent sophistication, are added to the mix. Predictably, the exuberance owners feel on launching yet another set of measures to their woebegone team soon evaporates when the team are on the receiving end of another reset to their targets and commission, coupled with an inference that everything they've done so far is wrong. Before you know it, you're back to where you started with just a tiny bit more evidence that your reasoning is off kilter regarding KPIs. How infuriating.

You get what you measure is undoubtedly a complicated recipe. Achieving the right balance of key ingredients is critical in determining whether turning up the heat under your sales team will deliver the potion you hope for.

9
Sales Myth #9: Sales People Are All A Bit Untrustworthy

One of the challenges we face working in the sales environment is that not everybody appreciates sales people. Thankfully, this doesn't often translate into an actual dislike of sales people, but many people have an inherent discomfort with what they expect a sales person to be doing. Perhaps the pinnacle of disdain is the expression of the 'snake oil salesman', which is widely understood to refer to someone selling a product or service that doesn't do what it's promised to do.

To this day one of the issues facing sales is its lack of professional qualification. In many people's perception, give someone the gift of the gab and a sharp suit and you have the stereotypical salesperson. Barriers to entry are low. We'd argue it takes years of study to become a good sales person, but crucially – unlike accountancy, law or medicine – it doesn't take long before you're allowed to get started.

As a matter of fact, neither of us would have ever anticipated a career in sales. The experience we'd had of sales at that formative age was limited to people who visited our homes trying to sell things we didn't need. When we left the north to head to uni, we'd have been given short shrift had we tried to explain to our parents we wanted our degrees to lead to sales careers. Yes, it was about numbers, but that didn't bestow on it the cachet or reputation of accountancy.

What's the story with snake oil?

Back in the late nineteenth century there was no such thing as trade descriptions legislation or an advertising watchdog; nor was there a pharmaceutical industry worthy of the name. Aspirin was only invented in 1899. Medicine was based on herbal remedies, potions and hubris. Many of the major brands we know today grew up during this period, frequently having been invented in a pharmacy or drug store with claims that suggested they were beneficial to health.

Pepsi, Coke and Dr Pepper all emerged from what we might now refer to as this nutraceutical environment, though with no health claims that would stand testimony today. Viewed from that angle, the only difference between Coke and snake oil is better marketing.[9]

In 1916 snake oil became something of an infamous case in the USA as its original founder, cowboy Clark Stanley, was charged and fined under the Pure Food and Drug Act[10] for misbranding and making false medicinal claims. The expression stuck, with the epithet of 'snake oil salesman' being one of the more disparaging remarks you might throw at a customer service executive, which is why sales people still tell us they dislike snake oil salesmen and can – with real emotion – explain how important it is for them not to be seen as one.

Nobody is happy with something they believe is snake oil but what stops this being simple is that we all have different ideas about what constitutes snake oil. Gerald Ratner's infamous boasting that many of the products his jewellers sold were 'total crap' sparked an irreversible change in fortunes for his high street chain.[11] All of us have hunches and prejudices and it's nice to have them confirmed, so when a polite and

---

9   'The history of Coca-Cola, Dr. Pepper and Pepsi', Pop Shop (no date), https://northmarketpopshop.com/history-of-coca-cola-dr-pepper-pepsi, accessed 14 January 2021

10   'Food and Drug Act of 1906', Encyclopaedia.com (updated 23 November 2020), www.encyclopedia.com/history/united-states-and-canada/us-history/food-and-drug-act-1906, accessed 23 November 2020

11   'The man who destroyed his multimillion dollar company in 10 seconds' [blog post], Business Blogs (no date), www.businessblogshub.com/2012/09/the-man-who-destroyed-his-multi-million-dollar-company-in-10-seconds/, accessed 23 November 2020

professional sales person reinforces that our purchase decision is right for us – 'It looks good on you' – we are pleased to hear it. Only later when our best (or worst) friends tell us that our haircut doesn't suit us or our new car isn't quartz blue – it's lilac – will we question whether we were mis-sold.

Economical with the truth

The challenge with calling out snake oil gets right to the truth that sales is all about people. It's an extraordinarily nuanced thing that can take on different meanings dependent on vocabulary, tone of voice and context. See what you think of the three perfectly innocent business scenarios below. They illustrate how what may seem like a reasonable business decision can be misinterpreted as sharp sales practice.

Scenario A

Cashflow is a nightmare for a small business and it's an unfortunate reality that you have to chase people to pay you on time. You can put late payment clauses into your terms and conditions, but in practice charging a client 2.5% extra for making you wait an extra month for your money isn't a way to boost sales. So, when a small business we know introduced new accounting software and was told it could stamp *overdue* in red letters across the bottom of each invoice they seized the opportunity. We all understand the problem and a gentle nudge doesn't hurt.

What happened

This was one of our suppliers. We had earlier joked with them about some sales consultants and what they referred to as 'snake oil salesmen'. In the context of a co-operative business relationship, we had all laughed about this as something we identified as happening to other people.

Nobody likes being on the receiving end of late payment, so we are scrupulous about paying people quickly. We often pay on receipt of invoice, rarely eating up the thirty days available before the due date, so when we received their first invoice, we felt quite uncomfortable about the *overdue* claim. Is it legal to issue a first invoice and claim it's overdue? Even HMRC doesn't do that, but short of exploring the legalities it just felt slippery. If felt like a sales trick.

In this case we get on well with that team and we laughed off the incident, but it's a living example of how something that is done with good intent can be re-imagined by the recipient as a pushy sales tactic.

Scenario B

A privately owned shop in a tourist resort has a disproportionately high number of visitors who don't buy. If they could charge a penny for just looking, business would boom. They have a carefully curated selection of gifts and curios from around £10 upwards but reckon they should stock a range of cheaper items to encourage more people to dig into their pockets. They find a local source of old glass jars, retro mugs and bottles that they buy for a few pounds. Artfully arranged in a large wicker basket, they hand-write a sign saying, 'All items £2' and wait for the coins to flow.

What happened

This happened to a friend of ours who was idling away his holiday on the south coast. As he describes his experience: 'I thought the shop was pricy, but fair enough, it was a tourist resort. Then I saw this basket full of junk and they were trying to charge me £2. That's when I knew they were ripping me off and I left.' Ouch.

Scenario C

An online provider of training and business support takes responsibility for delivering a government-sponsored initiative to grow business using 4G and 5G. Businesses innovating in this space will be able to access this training in a venue close to their office location, free of charge. Supported with EU funding, the campaign launches with a glossy website, smart analytics and an offer of training worth £1,000. What's not to like?

What happened

The organisation really struggled to encourage people to attend these training events. There was much to learn about how the booking process was handled and the online customer journey but in conversation with colleagues the simple feedback was, 'It's not really worth £1,000, is it?' Small business owners are swamped with high-quality sessions from reputable providers like banks, solicitors, Google, Facebook... There's a long list of corporates who want to connect with business owners and they'll run these events at a negligible cost. With resources like that it's no surprise the UK is so good at start-ups.

The £1,000 claim might have made a neat headline, but did it really stand scrutiny? A small business owner with that much to spend could source a full day of bespoke consultancy for their business and find a good number of highly qualified people willing to deliver it. This was offering two hours in a class-room with other people. It may well have cost £1,000 to set up and administer, but that didn't connect with the buyer's perceived value.

These three scenarios demonstrate how there can be a disconnect between seller and buyer. Nothing makes us think the seller set out to defraud or mislead but in each case the buyer perceived a little bit of trickery.

The Wild West of internet marketing

The overwhelming challenge we all face today is overcoming how the internet has spawned an entire host of snake oil sales people, promising the magic potions that will help business owners solve their sales problems and thereby strengthening this myth.

If you promote a product in Tesco, you have to reference the previous selling price. It must have been valid for twenty-eight days and there is copious regulation about how and when you can make these claims. Occasionally major retailers get caught out, but with tens of thousands of products on sale at any one time you can tell it's a mistake rather than sharp practice.

Contrast this with the internet. If you received a pound for every time you saw a consultancy proposition that promises, 'Sign up now and you'll receive this free training/book/widget worth £1,000,' you would be rich. It's not worth £1,000. They've never sold it for £1,000. They just made it up. They might not wear Stetsons these days, but snake oil sales people still exist.

Why does this matter to business owners? Because it's reputational. The examples above show how carefully you have to tread to sustain trust in your sales efforts. The priority you afford it is your choice. A small number of business owners will choose actions based simply on whether they make money. For them, self-esteem is measured in dollars and bragging rights, with community, the environment and reputation well down the list. They are not often people you'd choose to partner with. Most, though, instinctively grasp that reputation affects how your customers trust you, how long they stay with you and how easily you gain new ones. That reputation is the single most important factor in whether your business acquires the client list you think you deserve.

10

Sales Myth #10: I Need A Sales Person Urgently

You might have uttered these words and it's a request we hear with surprising frequency. A sales person is the external face of your company – someone who should understand your purpose, your culture and your product range, so the idea that someone can fulfil these roles urgently is one you might find curious.

In fact, when we hear this, our first thought is what exactly the business owner has done wrong. If you need an accountant urgently, or worse, a lawyer, then something has gone wrong. It's a good time to ask, 'What does this mean?'

There are certainly times when a business needs sales revenue urgently, although if you're in that situation we'd advise calling an accountant rather than a sales person. An accountant can make decisions that affect the profitability of your business tomorrow by cutting costs or renegotiating contracts and terms. A good sales person will take some time to become familiar with your business, their customer base and what ignites the space between the two. In the meantime, they're costing you money from day one. Revenues take longer.

We strongly argue that bringing a new sales person on board should be one of the more strategic decisions your business should take, not urgent in any respect. Start with a plan.

When do new sales people begin to pay back?

Virtually every sales person is brought on board with the intention of achieving growth either from new or existing customers, yet it's often not appreciated just how long it takes for that new person to deliver growth. Maybe we spend too long with accountants, but we're clear that the only surety of a sales person is that on day one you're paying their salary. Plus, they need a computer and possibly a car.

From day one it's a profit outflow and important for a business to understand how long it will take, or what sales level needs to be reached, before they break even and begin to contribute to your profit line.

'New recruits pay back in year one' is in fact Sales Myth #52. We've seen time and again – and often with high-profile businesses that should know better – that sales people are brought on board only for senior management to decide within twelve months that they are not delivering to the required level and letting them go. One international company we knew recruited a team of over twenty people and within a month of the last recruits joining announced a restructure, having miscalculated how quickly they could deliver to the bottom line.

A common mistake at this planning stage is to believe that key accounts offer a bigger opportunity than smaller customers. Managers are blinded by the dollar signs in their eyes, thinking the combination of bigger customers and their reps' bigger salaries will deliver bigger sales numbers. True, but only in part. The missing part of the equation is that it takes longer to influence these bigger customers to buy. The standards and systems they demand from you are more stringent than those of smaller customers. This in turn demands new skills of your senior team, new sales processes and often new systems. It can easily take three to five years to create a fully functioning Key Account Management (KAM) approach from a standing start.

If you've allocated budget for twelve months thinking that you'll dip a toe in the water with a team of KAMs you'll be disappointed. You'll waste the money you spend in year one and will create turmoil for your team and existing customers.

One medium-sized business we know of wanted to upskill their team of sales reps and put them all through a disruptive selection process to decide those who stayed. At the end of this the new team was recruited, with new job descriptions, KPIs, commission structures and targets. A residential induction programme lasted a fortnight. Quite naturally, it took over three months before they'd made first visits to customers, worked out the best routes around the territory, understood the products and made a few sales, and yet after nine months the senior team were asking what the ROI of the team was. With the new year budgets coming up they wanted to demonstrate a positive return on the cost of the team, without which they wouldn't get sign-off for next year.

There was no way this team had reached its full potential, so assessed on a few tentative steps in a new industry the whole group was disbanded. Careers disrupted, mortgages threatened and yes, there were some tears, all because the people at the top didn't understand the likelihood of achieving the objective.

LISTEN BEFORE YOU LEAP

We supported an agency in Kent called Chessboard to build their sales team. Charlotte had been made redundant from a job selling insurance renewals when her CV arrived. She was local, had sales experience, could start immediately and would be on three months' probation. If it didn't work out there was no risk. She joined the business two days later and was instantly given a list of lapsed clients to call with the intention of reawakening their enthusiasm for buying from Chessboard. Her induction was minimal, although she was shown where the teacups were hidden and how to access the CRM records.

Charlotte's impact was significant and immediate, but not in the way the business had hoped. We only found out about Charlotte after she joined, so we listened to her recorded calls. She was energetic and enthusiastic but accidentally managed to alienate, confuse or annoy many of the lapsed customers she spoke with. Her style, her tone of voice, her listening and her questioning skills all served to provoke negative responses. A neutral response leaving lapsed clients still lapsed or a friendly chat re-connecting them with the products and services of Chessboard would both have met the 'no risk' criteria upon which she was recruited, but she was a risk and the desire to recruit someone quickly had trumped the time taken to test whether she was suitable.

Getting back those lapsed customers may just have been made slightly harder by that decision. The sense of disappointment in the business was palpable. The whole sales team were looking forward to sharing the new leads Charlotte was going to provide. Instead, the

111

pressure was back on them. Not surprisingly, Charlotte was quickly let go. The sales team, recognising the impact that a failure to hit targets could deliver, started to ask, 'Who next?' The owner, of course, carried the disappointment of both the wasted wages and the lack of the expected boost to the sales line, with the sales team only too happy to concede that it was his fault for always jumping into things.

Our experience in designing sales organisations, just some of which we've described here, is why our instinctive reaction to someone asking for sales 'urgently' is that it's a response to some sort of crisis. On the contrary, for all the reasons outlined above, we see recruitment of sales personnel as a strategic decision. One it's important to get right – for you, your team and your recruits.

11
Sales Myth #11: I Can't Sell. Can You Help?

The truly weird thing about this statement is that you barely ever hear it from someone who's in the early days of a business, bumping along the bottom trying to earn a crust. Whenever someone tells us this it's invariably someone who has built a business from scratch and created a successful organisation, yet they can't sell.

We know a lady running a £1m business with a team of twelve people. She's personally recruited each of the team and brought in the contacts that have built up the business from zero. It's never polite to argue with potential clients so when she told us, 'I can't sell,' we were gobsmacked.

Everyone sells

We all sell, and we do it from an early age. Children are great at selling. Sometimes they peel away the buyer's resistance simply by using questions: 'Mummy, why can't I go to the park? Why? But why?' In adult life we're constantly pitching ideas – suggesting where we should go on holiday; persuading people to come to our parties; influencing colleagues on where to eat and what to drink. Because it comes intuitively, we don't think of this interaction as selling.

Over the years we've worked with numerous people who run franchises, often meeting them as they emerge from the dazzling journey of handing over their funding to buy the keys to a new adventure (or at least the handbook and some head office help). Many will tell us within the first sentence of an introduction that they can't sell. Their next words will then be all about how they raised the funds to buy into the group or persuaded their partner to forgo the certainty of a pension and spend it on this dream instead. And that's not selling?

We understand of course that this is different from being a professionally trained sales person, and if you find yourself in a position where you either have to recruit or manage sales people you may well feel that you're not equipped to untangle the knot in front of you. At this point, investing in someone who can help you write job ads, interview the best applicants and construct an onboarding programme could be money well spent but that's the technical aspect of selling.

Don't bring me down

What happens if you really don't believe you can sell? The relationship between our emotions, our behaviours and our thoughts are well-documented within clinical settings,[12] and this is no different. If your overriding belief is that you can't sell, being asked to sell is likely to trigger emotions that cause worry and nerves, leading to a reduction in your energy and efforts to avoid situations that cause you to try. This reinforces your original story about not being able to and the vicious circle continues, so beating an emotional hang-up of not being able to sell is an important issue to address.

THE 'CAN'T SELL' CONTAGION

Emma was a self-declared non-sales person. She had created a successful marketing agency from scratch and had a number of awards on her windowsill recognising her achievements. She had fifteen staff and a funky office space to be proud of, but in spite of evidence to the contrary, Emma 'couldn't sell'.

---

12 O Gough, 'Cognitive behavioural therapy can help manage stress at work', smallbusiness.co.uk (3 November 2016), https://smallbusiness.co.uk/behavioural-therapy-manages-stress-2534928, accessed 14 January 2021

Where that became more of an issue was how she unwittingly spoke about selling in front of her business and small sales team. They were regularly treated to Emma physically shuddering when she spoke about pitches to new clients and selling new ideas. Wholly inadvertently, she magnified all that could go wrong and why it would be hard to sell them an idea. She actively avoided having coaching conversations with her team and, in spite of her success, her words and narrative about all things sales-related painted a negative picture.

Emma's anxiety nurtured a team that hunkered down instead of reaching out to customers to explore their needs and successfully sell them solutions. Angst increased and rehearsals took far longer as people previously used to success prepared to fight off the risk of failure. Emma's indecision and fear of asking for a client's business began to affect how her team planned their presentations. Instead of punchy requests for business, sales pitches dissolved into vague, 'We're nice folks with nice ideas, what do you think?' endings. Pitches were lost to competitors.

Emma's business, her team and her results could all have been more impactful if she'd beaten the emotional hang-up of not being able to sell.

12
Sales Myth #12: The CRM System Will Tell Me That

If we ask clients whether their CRM system is about strategy or delivery, most would say it's about customer implementation. Getting the job done. Some would have a more strategic view of it and recognise its importance in planning, but this idea will rarely extend as far as marketing or brand development. Why would they need to use a CRM system when they are developing brand strategy?

Both views miss the point. More than anything, CRM is about people. Obviously, the information you capture with it is about people – it's about countless interactions between your teams and your customers, so at that level it's clearly about relationships, but deeper than this, the success and usefulness of a CRM is about your people and your culture.

As easy as ABC

We have a friend who's spent his working life running IT helpdesks for big corporates. If any job is guaranteed to question your belief that the customer is always right (Sales Myth #80), it's this one. Not one of us is immune from the irate call to the helpdesk about a malfunction that after much huffing and puffing is diagnosed as a user error. After decades of experience installing 'must have' new tech, one of our friend's great wisdoms is this: define the process before you buy the system.

So often we hear from small business owners who are disappointed with their CRM system. One company we came across spent £20,000 over a three-year period hoping for great things from Microsoft Dynamics. This figure is just the money handed over to the system provider. It doesn't include the cost of management time spent uploading spreadsheets, recoding data and trying to integrate email newsletters – all of it wasted when the system was scrapped after three years.

Sometimes we get to advise businesses before they install the system so can at least help them make informed choices. This is the stage at which the 'What does this mean?' is key. CRM systems are not all the same (and price points vary widely), so it's crucial to know what you want it to do before making the buying choice. Design the process before committing to the system.

We're only human

No CRM system will fix your sales process, engender teamwork or deliver a sales culture. It is not a cure-all for your sales performance or your management reporting. Why not? Because it's agnostic and it's inanimate.

Think about the Bible story of Noah and his ark. Facing a great flood, Noah rounded up animals of all sorts in pairs and corralled them onto his hastily constructed boat. One song's acknowledgement of the impracticalities of this enterprise was the 'great hippopotamus stuck in the door', but there is generally no recognition of the difficulties of capturing bees or pairing lions alongside sheep. It would have been total chaos.

That's what most businesses CRM systems are like. Built up over time, they contain a disparate series of data points, random and conflicting messages and pet projects.

When Noah floated back to dry land after forty days and was asked to prepare a management report on his journey, he would be forced to acknowledge the naughty monkey that was left behind, the issue between the fox and the hen, and that 'caterpillar problem'.

GARBAGE IN...

We're uncertain whether caterpillars were to blame for the demise of the market-leading CRM system within Chessboard, there were too many fingerprints to check. But die it did.

It had held tenure for over a decade. It was integrated across the entire business and many hours and much money had been spent creating bespoke reports and dashboards to guide management and board decisions. Licences were purchased and everyone was trained to use it. It was one person's job every month to extract and collate packs of management information for the board meeting. Whole days could be wasted looking for reasons why two columns of data appeared not to tally.

Eventually, but not before crucial decisions had been made, the quality of the data being held and the rigour with which it was being input came under scrutiny and were found wanting. Almost overnight the tool that had been the linchpin of the business had its reputation in ruins. Three months later it was being replaced by a competitor. Of course, the folks that filled it full of wonky data in the first place remained in situ. Busy fools.

Chessboard's realisation that they had created a team of busy fools lead to a feisty board meeting. Fingers were pointed and voices raised. After investing heavily in systems and people, the owners felt let down. How could senior managers have failed in their oversight of the team's activity and reporting?

For many businesses, their biggest cost is the cost of people, so getting best value for money from your investment in payroll is a critical objective. A CRM system working perfectly will facilitate exactly that, but if the base data isn't accurate, you'll get something different. Ask any user and they'll tell you completing CRM entries eats into their day job, so what you capture has to be insightful enough to balance out the extra workload. There is nothing wrong with CRM reports, they'll answer any question you pose, but the output is only ever as good as the data the system holds, and that's down to your people.

13
Sales Myth #13: I Know I Need To Be On Facebook

You might argue this is a marketing myth rather than a sales myth, but we unashamedly include it here for two good reasons. Firstly, it's all your money, so if you're spending on Facebook to drum up sales leads then you're not spending it on more traditional sales and marketing methods. Secondly, this type of statement is one of the clearest examples we hear of the 'What does this mean?' being lost. It doesn't matter whether this comment is made about Facebook, about digital marketing or about the billboard outside your office. Unless you've done some smart thinking, you don't know you need to be there at all.

There are of course plenty of people who will say you should have a presence on Facebook or other social media, but those who inhabit the 24/7 social media world we live in would tell you that, wouldn't they? More than anything, this myth is a victory for tactics over substance.

Spend your money wisely and spend it only once

Let's go back to the first reason we include it. Over the years we have heard sales people in some well-regarded businesses give away discount to a customer with the words, 'Yes, you can have that; it comes from the marketing budget.' It drives us mad. When you're running a business, it doesn't matter what pot the funds come from – it's your money. It perhaps demonstrates how cocooned from reality some employees in these larger organisations have become.

Any expenditure comes out of your company P&L and can only be spent once. If it's spent on your cheap deal today, then it can't fund tomorrow's magazine ads or your next sales bonus, so any sales and marketing expenditure should have a prickly, 'What does this mean?' preceding it. Who precisely do you want to do what?

We recognise that going against the flow in these situations is tough. It's not easy to explain to your shareholders, accountant or muse that you're not doing social media, the exhibition stand or AdWords this year when the sales fairy is whispering that everyone else is.

If you've thought about the value proposition of your product or service and know that one of your target groups is accountants within ten miles of your office or if you know you want them to attend a tax seminar you're holding next month, then advertising to them on Facebook could be a wise move.

There are alternatives: you could write to all the accountants locally, hoping a hand-addressed letter achieves more than a social media post (it probably does). You could email them if you have email addresses. You could connect on LinkedIn. There is no shortage of possible tactics, and only testing a few will prove which works best but you can at least prioritise because you have a clear idea of who (accountants) you want to do what (attend the seminar). Apply this level of scrutiny to all your sales activities.

WE'VE ALWAYS DONE THIS

One small design company we worked with had always exhibited at an annual building convention. Marketing materials and the stand at the show cost almost £25,000. The entire office ground to a halt for the month before the show as hundreds of bags of brochures were packed up. The MD complained for the other eleven months of the year about visitors requesting information at the show but not buying.

The owner of the business was paralysed by this indecision. Worrying that the company 'couldn't not attend' but resentful that every year it did, she was the rabbit caught in bright headlights. Every year the stress this engendered began to seep throughout the commercial team.

When we really scrutinised the 'What does this mean?' in this case, we established that the company marketing team wanted influential architects to recommend their products. The people attending their stand were mainly home owners reading about their dream home and enjoying a day out at the NEC. The expensive stand was entertaining the wrong audience.

Why did they exhibit at this show? Because they 'knew' they had to do it. Within twelve months of us being involved they had pulled out. Any negative sales impact? No. Management impact? A team of people who were now much more engaged, knowing they were focusing on the activities that would really make a difference to sales.

14

Sales Myth #14: Customers? That's Sales' Job

This is one of the more dangerous myths. Dangerous because in some businesses it's no longer a myth – it's become the standard way of operating.

At its lowest level it starts as an admin thing. A query comes in and whoever fields it first sees a customer angle and passes it to sales. It's the right thing to do. It's as the company scales and the issues grow that it presents a problem. Before you know it, consumers are the sole domain of marketing, money is the job of finance and anything to do with shifting product is about supply chain. Except the customer doesn't see it this way.

The customer cares about outputs. They're not interested in your internal functions, job descriptions or anniversary celebrations. They want to know what you can deliver to them – its quality, reliability and price. What you do for them is paramount. What drives you, your purpose, is interesting. How you comply with relevant legislation, manage extended supply chains and respect the environment is increasingly important. In terms of internal process and job descriptions, how you do it is pretty much irrelevant.

We've seen no evidence of a big company/little company correlation to this myth. We've met small businesses where the founder's early passion for their customers hasn't gone away, so they still act as the ticking heartbeat of the customer organisation. Yet we've also seen some where lack of meaningful engagement with customers has resulted in a bunker mentality, with a focus on internal policies and process.

Regardless of scale, you should beware if you're selling a complicated technical product such as software or healthcare. It's all too easy for the focus to end up on the item itself rather than on the customer or patient.

LOST IN TRANSLATION

Interrogate's technology was complicated. Not complicated to use, but certainly to amend and recode or to untangle if it decided to misbehave.

They prided themselves on having a great set of developers and a tech team that could beat any of their competitors. The sales team had a working knowledge of each system and were highly competent at demonstrating the value of each to clients. It wasn't their job, however, to fix bugs and resolve coding issues – that was when one of the tech team was required to take off their headphones and help. That's when it often got tricky.

Helen was part of this team and knew her code and her product inside out. She resisted being involved with clients at all cost. Warren was the account manager trying to resolve a long-standing problem for one of his clients. He'd been the translator of messages between Helen and her equivalent in his client's organisation for six weeks. Helen had sent emails, told him what to say and provided screenshots, all the while steadfastly refusing to speak with the client. That was sales' job, not hers.

Helen's client got more confused and more frustrated, straining what was a long-standing and fruitful relationship. Helen knew that six weeks was an unacceptably long time to leave a client waiting for a fix, but didn't connect this with her refusal to participate in what she believed was a sales problem.

Eventually, after intervention by the MD and with some behind-the-scenes coaching, Helen joined a telephone call to the client. Warren did the introductions and managed the call, promising to take over any sticky comments made about how long this had taken to resolve. Fifteen minutes of technical speak (some jargon that bamboozled Warren); two amendments of code; a

> test in a sandbox and order was restored. A happy client subsequently went on to order the enhanced version of the same system.

Strangely, we all know what it's like to be on the receiving end of this disconnected customer service, but it doesn't always translate into action. The frustration we feel when our home Wi-Fi drops and nobody at the broadband provider cares; the anger when an airline leaves you stranded in Heathrow for four hours after a technical delay. It's easy in these situations to see the customer perspective, but it's often simply not on the radar of internal teams to start with the customer benefit and work back from there.

As a business owner, this drives you nuts. You know your team members choose where to spend their hard-earned salary based on their customer experience, yet somehow this doesn't translate into what they do with your customers. You've struggled for years to deliver on promises with these customers, yet your team members can damage your reputation in minutes because 'it's not my job'.

Selling is everyone's job.

At the heart of this is what is meant by sales. Sales (with a capital S) is a function. Whether it's one person or one hundred, they've hopefully been equipped with sales skills and are usually the first point of contact between a business and its customers.

Selling, on the other hand, is a way of life. It's the job of everyone in the organisation. That doesn't mean everyone needs to visit customers or go on sales training days. It just means they need to understand that everything they do is designed to improve the customer experience. It's all about the customer.

15
Sales Myth #15: We'd Be Alright If It Wasn't For Customers

Have you had days when you felt like this? We first heard this sentiment from the finance director of Veggboxx after a meeting where the sales manager had set out the current commercial performance and the risks and opportunities facing the business. In summary, sales were stable, the team were performing well and some margin efficiencies had been built into this year's plan, but the market was becoming more demanding, so future growth would be tough.

The emotion behind the FD's comment was one of frustration that, despite doing the right things internally, they couldn't rely on their customers to give them the kudos they might expect for doing so. Translation: they weren't getting the sales they deserved.

What made this a myth? When we helped Veggboxx assess the market share position, we established theirs was a product group that was delivering low growth. The UK market is mature and unless you're selling breakthrough products, there are few double-digit growth opportunities left.

Nonetheless, the market was predicted to grow maybe as much as 5% that year, with their company remaining flat. If this was the fault of customers, how was it that their competitors seemed to be navigating the retail minefield more successfully than them? On closer inspection we discovered that they had been clawing back marketing expenditure for years. It had begun innocently enough. As costs had risen, they had nudged down advertising spend. The money spent on consumers was declining. The business was doing the right things, but it was doing less of them.

It's funny how time flies in business, so over a few years this had created a sort of bunker mentality. Customers were out to get them. Trying to damage their business by getting one over on them. It's something we see surprisingly often. The problem with this siege mindset is that there's no counterbalance. The customer doesn't sit in your internal meetings explaining why they are being reasonable and actually you're not quite aligned with their primary growth strategies. Not persuading critical customers to buy when you want them to, feels like a loss of control over the business. Resentment seeps in as investment decisions are paused. The feeling persists until it's all-pervading. Look at these businesses from a distance and you see the real emotion – even anger – that the team express when talking about 'customer X'.

In reality, few suppliers get as much of their customer time and attention as they would like. Customers don't care as much about your product or service as you think they should. We've occasionally seen a situation where a buyer consciously makes a decision to detriment a specific supplier. It could be triggered by corporate manoeuvres like an attempted take-over or it could be a result of a perceived personal slight from a dodgy salesperson. Usually, though, the customer just can't be bothered. They are every bit as busy as you and will make decisions that work for them. Precious few suppliers will come to be seen as preferred partners, but by and large, burning extra energy on whether they proactively help or hinder your business simply isn't on their radar.

If your customer's not excited by you, that's because your value proposition isn't exciting to them. This was summed up by the CEO of a dental company we worked with. He ran a highly geared, venture-backed business. His company made toothbrushes, but his business was growth. He explained that if his sales people tell him the customer isn't buying, he gets on their backs. If they can't persuade the customer to say yes, then they haven't tried hard enough – they haven't found the solution that makes the customer want to buy.

This is a two-way thing of course. Back to Gerald Ratner – if your product is 'total crap' then you have a lot of work to do internally before your customer will thank you for it. There's this continual evolution of exploring the value your product or service adds to your customer and tweaking your proposition to relentlessly enhance it. None of us can do without customers and every aspect of our business needs to be built around this value proposition. We have to make it easier for them to say yes.

16

Sales Myth #16: Couldn't We Double Our Sales Just By Improving Conversion Rates?

For most businesses conversion rates are less than 50%, which to any manager looks as though money is being left on the table. If we could only increase conversion rates… Arithmetically of course, the answer is yes. If everything else remained the same (though we'll come onto how big an *if* this is) and conversion rates doubled, then sales would be twice what they are today. Result.

Let's wind back and make sure we're clear about terminology. Conversion rate is the proportion of actions that result in a given output. It doesn't have to be about sales. Jonny Wilkinson, rugby union legend and winner of the 2003 World Cup with England had a kick conversion rate of around 86%. Out of every 100 kicks he took, he scored with 86.[13]

The principle can be applied to any level of the sales process. You could measure the number of initial enquiries that lead to a meeting; the number of meetings that lead to a full product demonstration; the number of demos that lead to a quote or the number of quotes that lead to a sale. At a high level, one of the critical conversion measures is how many leads convert to a sale.

A small number of industries sell products that are unique, resulting in high conversion rates, but this is the conversion measure that generally turns out below 50%. Often a long way below. At the time of writing, our clients' conversion rates spread between 5% and 50% – with most towards the lower end. The one outlier at 50% only follows up leads that are referrals from existing clients. Less reliable lead-generation methods involving cold-calling could be as low as 1% or 2%.

$$\text{Conversion rate} = \frac{\text{number of orders}}{\text{number of leads}}$$

$$\frac{20 \text{ orders}}{100 \text{ leads}} = 20\% \text{ conversion}$$

---

13 'The Kicking Divide Between Hemispheres' [blog post], Linebreak Rugby (June 2016), http://linebreakrugby.com/2016/06/rugby-kicking-stats, accessed 23 November 2020

The second factor that's critical to consider is the cost of an order. This is calculated as follows:

$$\text{Cost of order} = \frac{\text{cost of lead}}{\text{conversion rate}}$$

$$\frac{\text{Lead cost £100}}{\text{Conversion rate 20\%}} = \text{£500 cost of order}$$

At this point it's worth thinking about Jonny Wilkinson again. Obviously, you can't double a conversion rate of 86%. For all the hyperbole beloved of sports coaches and commentators it's not possible to give 101%, but let's say we wanted to make Jonny Wilkinson 10% better by improving his conversion rate to 94.6%. That's 10% more points, right?

Well… *If* everything else stays the same.

With Jonny, the value of a kick is 2.58 points: the 'lead' of a penalty is worth 3 points and he converts at 86%, so each kick is worth 2.58 (3 × 86). Except not all leads are the same value. A penalty is worth 3 points, whereas a conversion is worth just 2. That really complicates the calculation.

Then consider the difficulty of each kick. If Jonny took only kicks directly in front of the posts, he'd have a conversion rate nearer to 100%. Conversely, if he regularly attempted strikes from his own half the 86% might seem optimistic. What about the side of the pitch he kicks from? Every individual has a tendency towards right or left, so that would affect conversion rates. Sales people, in just the same way, will have natural tendencies that help them succeed in certain circumstances.

How would we factor in the importance of the occasion? Isn't it easier to slot over kicks when England are leading Georgia by 50 points in a friendly than lining up a 79th-minute winner in the Six Nations?

The idea that a conversion rate is something that exists in isolation is quite fanciful. Yes, it can be improved, but doing so has implications in other parts of the business.

This is made worse if it's used as a key measure. Imagine Jonny was bonused on conversion rate. He becomes interested only in easy kicks from in front of the posts. When a penalty is given near the touchline, he 'takes a knock' and leaves the kick to one of his colleagues. Note how this predetermines the reserve kicker to have a much worse conversion rate, making Jonny look even better. His reputation is enhanced while sitting on the turf having a rub from the physio.

Then, because conversion rate isn't quite working out, the team realise they must score all their tries under the posts. Any easy scoring opportunities in the corner are sacrificed so that Jonny can preserve his 100% record. England become a dull, low-scoring team where their plan is to drive big blokes down the middle with Jonny converting simple kicks.

This might sound a bit far-fetched, but we've seen similar situations arise in businesses where conversion rate has been treated as a goal in itself:

- Companies where the conversion rate percentage drops as the business grows rapidly (in some categories AdWords can only provide a certain number of easy kicks).

- Companies where junior sales people convert large numbers of small orders because they're the easy ones.

- Companies where senior reps ringfence leads so they win the accolade of repeat orders.

This can be intensely frustrating for business owners. The opportunity looks a big one, and driven by the urge to act, they seize on what looks like a simple solution only to find the outcome causes problems elsewhere. Every failed initiative is a learning opportunity, but this doesn't easily offset feelings of regret that come with knowing you spent time and money on a tactical and short-term initiative.

Improving conversion rates is worthwhile but focusing *just* on improving conversion rate without anticipating its impact elsewhere is something that is likely to tighten the tangle in your sales performance rather than unravel it.

Conclusion

Everyone loves a good story, so listening to sales myths is not inherently damaging; but like the sirens luring sailors towards the rocks with their hypnotic songs, they are dangerous if you follow them. The bigger problem is that you rarely hear them alone.

What often happens in a business is that the view of sales is coloured by a tangled mix of these half-truths and rumours. Over time this leads to frustration about disappointing sales results and underperforming sales people on the one hand, and distrust about out-of-touch leadership on the other.

Quick fixes like sales training and DiSC personality profiles have been tried, all of which cost a measurable chunk of money but all of which eventually ended up in a desk drawer somewhere. Occasionally it culminates in the biggest tangle of all: firing the sales manager.

Now the business is faced with a tricky conundrum of how to fix the performance problems. How to extract truth from myth; how to re-engage the team; how to reignite results. It's all become one anxious tangle, where pulling the first visible loose end seems only to tighten the knot.

It's a nightmare. It's real. And you're in the lead role.

PART TWO

BRINGING SOLUTIONS TO LIFE

Introduction: Solutions

Did you read the whole of Part One or did you just pick out the chapters that most interested you and jump here to find the answer? Many business owners are impatient for results but deep down most of them know that doing the right thing is better than doing the easiest thing. Adopting a rounded approach to answering the questions that concern most business owners can help you create a successful outcome from each business challenge.

Ask yourself how you can combine the three angles of planning, people and implementation to deliver robust solutions: practical plans, motivated people and committed follow-through. And keep asking,

'What does this mean?' So many business initiatives wither before they've ever really gained momentum. We're not easily duped by a high-powered project title, and nor should you be.

17
Why Do We Do This?

There's a long-standing joke about productivity which originates from the US. Reportedly, a government auditor turned up at a business to conduct a tax assessment only to find a large building containing a small number of desks. Surprised, the auditor asked, 'How many people work here?' to which the manager replied, 'About half of them.'

It's an adage that holds true to this day. In any workplace there are people who routinely go the extra mile to make things happen for the business, for their boss or for their customers, but how many people do you know who turn up for work each day because they must? People who are uninspired by their work, people who are waiting for that happy day when their pension kicks in, or people who just don't get on with the boss.

We've heard from numerous people in senior roles who are not really excited by the job, but with teenage children and university fees looming they make comments like, 'I'm not going until they offer me the package.' The business ploughs on, blissfully unaware of this underlying level of disengagement. It's not great for the organisation and worse for the individual. Remember: 'One life. Live it.'

What was the trigger that caused you to make your biggest career change?

We're not talking about a new job with more money. We mean that fundamental change when you exited corporate life or the day you walked away from years of accountancy training to do something you're actually passionate about. Remember the feeling of exhilaration that came with it? Not surprisingly, numerous surveys report disturbingly high dissatisfaction in the workplace. Work by Mercer Human Resource Consulting in January 2019 showed that only 64% of workers in the UK are satisfied with their job.[14] It's not an unusual level. Occasionally circumstances such as Brexit or the coronavirus pandemic will result in people taking whatever work they can

---

14 'Survey shows UK job satisfaction and commitment on the decline' (AMA, 24 January 2019), www.amanet.org/articles/survey-shows-uk-job-satisfaction-and-commitment-on-the-decline, accessed 14 January 2021

find in the short term, but as the economy recovers the satisfaction level will impact employees' willingness to hang around.

Employees have long been expressing greater expectations that the business they work for stands for something and the strains of 2020 have simply accelerated the number of people thinking this way. The final vestiges of the job-for-life concept disappeared with the Great Recession, but for many of today's employees that's the last thing they would want anyway.

We remember recruitment procedures that were all about the hiring company, but in today's social and economic environment the rules have changed. It's still about recruiting and retaining the talent that's crucial to the success of your business, but engaging and inspiring the workforce is a key part of making your company somewhere people aspire to work.

These are some of the factors driving businesses to think about purpose.

The importance of purpose

There is a plethora of data now available that shows just how important this is becoming in the minds of consumers. Accenture's report *To Affinity and Beyond:*

From me to we, the rise of the purpose-led brand, commissioned in late 2018, reports some of the key metrics:

- 66% say it's important that a company is transparent with where it sources its materials, how it treats employees fairly, etc.
- 53% say that companies that actively communicate their purpose are more appealing than those that do not.
- 52% of UK consumers want companies to take a stand on an issue close to their heart.[15]

Not surprisingly, the strength of consumer feeling in turn drives economic benefits. Again, there is much research into this, with *Harvard Business Review*'s report *The Business Case for Purpose* one that provides useful statistics. Those businesses who considered themselves as prioritising purpose achieved higher growth than those that didn't: 58% of 'prioritisers' achieved double-digit growth compared to 42% of 'laggards'. The picture is the same in their respective abilities to transform and innovate.[16]

The expectations of leaders in these businesses are high:

---

15 *To Affinity and Beyond: From me to we, the rise of the purpose-led brand* (Accenture Strategy, 2018), www.accenture.com/_acnmedia/ Thought-Leadership-Assets/PDF/Accenture-CompetitiveAgility-GCPR-POV.pdf, accessed 23 November 2020
16 *The Business Case For Purpose* (*Harvard Business Review*, 2015), www. hbr.org/resources/pdfs/comm/ey/19392HBRReportEY.pdf, accessed 23 November 2020

- 89% believe purpose will deliver employee satisfaction.

- 85% would recommend a business with purpose to others.

- 80% believe a business with purpose will have greater loyalty.

What is purpose?

Purpose in a company context is about representing something bigger than the business – a higher goal than your range of products and services can deliver today. Some say it's a touchpoint that should deliberately be unattainable – something your business will still be standing for and striving for in a hundred years. Contrast that with strategy, which at longest is likely to be three to five years.

A purpose needs to be captured in simple, short language and trigger emotion. As an illustration, here are the Purpose/Mission statements from three global manufacturers of trainers:

- 'To be the global leader in the sporting goods industry with brands built on a passion for sports and a sporting lifestyle. We are committed to continuously strengthening our brands and products to improve our competitive position.'

- 'To become the number one brand for the sports enthusiast. To accomplish this, we pledge to continue to make the best product; striving to build upon our technological advances and pushing the limits on what we can learn from the body and its needs in athletic gear.'

- 'To bring inspiration and innovation to every athlete in the world. If you have a body, you are an athlete.'

Any guesses? The first, somewhat Germanic version, is Adidas.[17] The second is Asics,[18] a brand often chosen by real runners ahead of their more mainstream competitors. The last is Nike.[19]

All three tick the box of describing a higher vision that is unlikely to ever be finished. The first two, though, make the internally focused mistake of setting the context as being the global leader. No consumer cares about that. It's only really the third one that sets a noble mission that connects with people emotionally. It's not just about those with athletic prowess – this purpose is for the world. All nations, all ages and fitness levels can take some motivation from this to get off the starting line.

Where purpose really counts is in how it's delivered. The words are meaningless without action, commit-

---

17 www.mission-statement.com/adidas, accessed 23 November 2020
18 www.asics.com/ca/en-ca/about-us, accessed 23 November 2020
19 www.about.nike.com, accessed 23 November 2020

ment and follow-through, but really only one of these three has the communicative power to mobilise customers.

Simon Sinek is a renowned author and speaker on the topic of purpose. His core principle, and the title of one of his books, is to 'start with why'.[20] Like all terminology around company mission, strategy and goals there are debates about vocabulary. For simplicity we consider mission the same as purpose. They are both about the 'why' of your business and both set long-term aspirations that will probably never be fully delivered.

What you do and how you do it are important considerations. Imagine you're a manufacturer of building materials. You're in the construction industry (what) and you provide better customer service than any of your competitors (how). Purpose can take you onto a different level, though. Say your purpose became 'Building better homes for Britain'. Customer service doesn't become less important (you can't build better homes if contractors are standing idle on building sites waiting for your delivery). The commitment to why, though, opens up a range of different areas in which you can excel. Maybe you create a charter helping the public understand the quality of their homes. Perhaps you introduce measures of wellbeing into the homes you build (architects are already discussing this, so it's not as far-fetched as it might sound). Perhaps you

---

20   S Sinek, *Start With Why: How great leaders inspire everyone to take action* (Penguin, 2011)

source all your materials from sustainable sources or commit to erecting a proportion of properties that are carbon-neutral.

Ella's Kitchen, a manufacturer of baby food in the UK and a certified B Corp, makes a big play on the importance of purpose. Their mission isn't to be the UK's biggest baby food manufacturer but 'To improve children's lives through developing healthy relationships with food'.[21] It's another example of something that will never have a tick in the completed box – there will always be more to do. It also satisfies the criteria of being set out in a few simple, clear words. The power of this purpose stretches way beyond simply selling more boxes. Which do you think is the most compelling for customers: Ella's 'creating healthy eating habits that last a lifetime' or Adidas being 'global leader in the sporting goods industry'?

How and what you do is figured out through strategy, but with purpose you're already thinking bigger than being just a factory making baby food, running shoes or electrical cable. All the evidence is that consumers are heading that way and there is commercial benefit in being able to delight and surprise them by being there too.

---

21 Ella's Kitchen, www.ellaskitchen.co.uk/sustainability/ #!#sustainability-our-mission, accessed 23 November 2020

How does corporate social responsibility (CSR) fit into this?

There is some scepticism about whether CSR is really a game-changer, not least because it sounds like company jargon. Have you ever seen a large corporate claiming to do good and thought it's just green-wash? Corporates doing good are always going to raise some eyebrows about banner-waving. Does it really run deep, or does it stop at some superficial charity work that doesn't materially move the dial?

We work with businesses both large and small and with a few notable exceptions we'd say purpose really permeates smaller outfits. Sure, companies like Ella's Kitchen and Innocent – both accredited B Corps – are truly committed to developing communities and protecting the environment, but for most corporates CSR is like the merry-go-round. When the music stops, it ends.

CSR overlaps with purpose but isn't quite the same thing. If you have a strong purpose, it's likely that you'll be undertaking some activities that would qualify as CSR. If you're 'Building better homes for Britain' you're probably doing something about the health and diversity of workers in the sector or improving your impact on the environment. On the other hand, you could do these things under the guise of CSR without really having a clear and simple business purpose.

This brings us to the heart of purpose and CSR. If every corporation in the UK encourages its staff to raise funds for community projects and gives them a day off each year for charity projects, then the world is a better place. Many businesses, large and small, are going beyond this and really thinking about how they can engage more proactively and regularly with their employees and communities. For businesses that choose this route it's critical that they really mean it. Sometimes the challenge comes when they are perceived to be jumping on a bandwagon – the backlash over Pepsi's advert with Kendall Jenner being a case in point.[22] Other businesses are exposed when money gets in the way. As has been pointed out many times, principles are only principles when they cost you something. Go back to Accenture's report: 62% of people expect a brand to have ethical values and demonstrate authenticity in everything it does. You cannot fake purpose.

Should we have company values?

For a small business, whether you document values should really be optional. It only becomes important when you're recruiting and someone asks what the company culture is like. Answer that with your personal opinion and you run the risk that inconsistency is creeping in. If it's not documented, can you

22   D Quenqua, 'Pepsi says "sorry" and removed Kendall Jenner ad from the web', *PR Week* (5 April 2017), www.prweek.com/article/1429761/pepsi-says-sorry-removes-kendall-jenner-ad-web, accessed 14 January 2021

be sure everyone has bought into the same standards? Pause for a minute and ask yourself how clear your business values are. Could all your team members explain them?

We've experienced large organisations where values are nothing more than wallpaper. Literally, given the amount of money spent on internal poster campaigns. Managers can – and sometimes do – bang on about them at conferences, but most employees struggle to name them. Not that they don't have values personally and we're sure most employees do the right thing, they're just not lined up and interpreted as management expects.

If you're reaching the stage where you want to capture values, then we advise three steps:

Firstly, engage the team in creating them. If you capture what people already think is great about being in the organisation and what makes you unique, then your chances of having them buy into them later are vastly enhanced.

Secondly, capture details and examples of what's in and what's not. Facilitate that first conversation with Post-its and flipcharts and save the exact quotes. A headline of Trust or Integrity will soon be forgotten if people can't be held to account for specific behaviours that support or refute the values.

Which leads us onto the third and maybe most important point. Give employees a way to question the values. It can be quite uncomfortable, but if you claim to operate with integrity, then your team need to know they can ask why you're holding back information from a customer about a production crisis. Values can easily wither and die, so allowing the team to express their surprise that certain policies might not fit with the published values is crucial to keeping them flourishing. It is also an opportunity to restate the importance of your purpose.

Will purpose make me money?

Just reading this question in black and white should be enough for you to appreciate how misplaced it is. When you find your purpose – either in business or in life – then you'll pursue it with an intensity and commitment that renders this question irrelevant. You can't fake purpose. In fact, there's a strong argument that a business only gets to demonstrate purpose when it costs them money. Up to that point it's just business as usual.

It's perhaps easier to demonstrate in a non-work context. Ask people what drives them and for many the answer will be some form of purpose statement: 'I want to be the best parent I can be,' or, 'I want to give my children the best start in life,' or, 'I want to become something my parents can be proud of.' Nobody would attempt to strengthen the impact of these goals by adding the words, '…as long as it doesn't cost me anything.' We all know that these high-level aims imply sacrifice and effort. It's the fact they don't come free that makes them worth the strain.

The potential upside is that doing the right thing is becoming increasingly attractive in a business context. Conversely, the downside of chasing profit at the expense of demonstrating values can be expensive. When Boohoo was exposed as sourcing garments from sweatshops in Leicester paying below minimum wage, their share price collapsed over 30% in a matter of days, wiping millions from the company's valuation.[23]

Purpose can make your business more attractive: to customers, your team and to investors. By establishing continuity in what you do and why you do it, you build resilience into your organisation's DNA, but recognise that profit isn't a reason for establishing purpose. Purpose is the why and the journey will never end, but it's a route worth travelling.

---

23   R Davies and A Kelly, 'More than £1bn wiped off Boohoo value as it investigates Leicester factory', *The Guardian* (6 July 2020), www.theguardian.com/business/2020/jul/06/boohoo-leicester-factory-conditions-covid-19, accessed 14 January 2021

18
Can You Help Me Get The Customers I Deserve?

Getting the customers a business deserves is perhaps the most recurring theme of the work we do with clients, partly because it's made up of many interwoven themes. Scrutinise the question though, and it becomes clear it's a double-edged sword. Many businesses will believe they don't have the customers they deserve – yet – but many customers are convinced their suppliers receive exactly what they deserve.

Success in this area is thus not just about pushing conversations harder or knocking on more doors, it's about honestly assessing what you do inside your business that makes you better and more compelling in the eyes of your customers. Dial up the capability around 'deserve' and the customers will follow. Do you honestly deserve more than you currently get?

How do your customers rate you?

A good place to begin here is to ask what measures you can identify that prove a customer rates you more highly than your competition. It's probably not sales.

A growing sales number is a sign of a healthy business and it's vitally important to you, but if you're growing behind the market it's quite clear your customers don't value you highly enough. Market share might be a better indicator, but in many industries this doesn't exist. Besides, it can be distorted by price variations, advertising and various other factors.

In some industries you can measure yourself by industry surveys or you might compile your own customer feedback. You might operate in a market where customers designate partner suppliers so you can measure yourself by your success in achieving partner status.

You might be able to extract a key step in your sales funnel and use that as a benchmark. The number of quotes you're able to convert to sales, for instance, would give you an idea of how highly your customers rated their customer experience with you.

In practice, though, most of these metrics are imperfect in one way or another, so the ideal approach is to take three or four and run them in parallel to give an overall health check. Develop a paranoia about whether your key customers – when pushed – will bring an opportunity to you or your competition.

One business owner explained a measure that was highly relevant to her industry. Customers in that market typically bought on an ad hoc basis and usually following a Google search. Repeat rates were low. One of the major players in this sector published its customer retention rate in its annual report. It was around 20% higher than her own. This became a fixation for her. She – rightly – identified it not just as a way of making her business more profitable, but as an important indicator of how valued her business was by customers.

In your industry it might be no more accurate than a judgement call around some indicators, but if that's the case it's probably a judgement call for your customer too, so keep this relentless focus on reading their intentions.

How are you different?

Be tough with yourself about your point of difference and measure it. You might be producing a unique organic yoghurt that's flavoured with Sicilian lemons, but how big is that segment of the market? How many people are prepared to spend extra on organic yoghurt? How many care that your lemons are from a remote farmstead off the coast of Italy and will subsidise your dream instead of just picking up the biggest grocery brand?

Smart buyers looking for improved commercial terms will of course tell you your product is too similar to something they already stock, just a copycat, but the painful truth of most markets is that suppliers do overestimate how distinctive they are in the eyes of buyers.

You don't get much more distinctive than a London black cab. Truly iconic. Yet they failed entirely to recognise that customers no longer saw them as distinctive. The vehicle itself is unique enough, but they weren't differentiated enough on their core offering – getting you from A to B – to resist Uber when they arrived in the UK. Black cab drivers also had a point of distinction in that they are required to pass 'The Knowledge of London' test – a comprehensive assessment of their ability to navigate the backstreets of London in the shortest possible time – and expected to memorise around 25,000 streets in the capital. Except, with the advent of satnav, the benefit of this distinctiveness disappeared almost overnight.

Why would a paying customer see exceptional value in an iconic vehicle and a churlish driver with a great memory (they never pretended customer service was part of their distinctiveness) when you can order an Uber on a predictable schedule at a cheaper price?

There is massive benefit in asking existing customers what they value most about you and where they would choose you ahead of the competition. It's frequently not what you most expect, so be tough on yourself to identify your true point of difference. Monitor the competition (Google Alerts is free and simple to set up), monitor industry trends for the risk of disruption and really listen to your customers.

Customer personas

It's valuable to create customer personas for your main customer types. If your business is conducted through a small number of key accounts the first part of this isn't necessary: you will know your key contacts as individuals with names and personalities, so no need to profile them this way.

Where you have a significant number of customers though, it's useful to think about the types of customers you have (or wish to have). Aim for between three to five different types. If you're feeling creative, you can create visuals of them and give them names. It's a bit of fun and can be useful in helping you bring them to life.

Begin with some basic demographic and company information. Typically, what age and gender might they be and what sort of income bracket? What size of company measured by turnover or number of employees? What part of the country?

More revealing is when you move onto exploring people's emotions and behaviours. What problem is your ideal customer trying to fix? They could be asking for a price for buying branded hats from you, but these might be for an overseas conference for 500 people. The hat isn't the issue – providing a memorable experience is. So how can you help with that? What impact will it have for the decision-maker if you can't deliver for them? If it's supplying hats, they'll go somewhere else, but not every problem is solved that easily. What knock-on effects might it have, like slowing production, letting down customers or making them look bad in front of management?

A good way of capturing this is in an empathy map, where you consider what your buyer is seeing, thinking, doing and feeling. See the example empathy map below.

There are numerous free templates online that enable you to create customer personas once you've worked out some of the key attributes you're seeking in a customer. If you're excited about a particular format, then run with that one, but the importance lies in the thinking and insight rather than the layout.

What do they think and feel?	What do they see?
• Key factors	• Market environment
• Hopes and concerns	• Friends and colleagues
• Etc	• Etc
What do they hear?	**What do they say and do?**
• Influencers	• Business behaviour
• Competitors	• Appearance
• Etc	• Etc
Pain	**Gain**
• Barriers to success	• Wants and needs
• Frustrations	• Measures of success
• Etc	• Etc

Doing this exercise thoroughly can be time-consuming but it will reward you in focusing your strategic decisions about who you want to target and where you will spend to reach them. It's also particularly valuable as you grow the organisation and need to explain to others what you are about. Whether it's employees, sales agencies or use of AdWords and Facebook, being clear on the type of customer you're targeting helps with explaining your motives to this wider group.

Exciting your customers

The final aspect of acquiring the customers you deserve is about how you excite your customers. Really, this is a combination of the factors above and is summarised neatly in the comment, 'It's all about the customer, stupid.'

For all the great work done every day in companies throughout the world, most companies get the customers they deserve. It might not feel that way, but it often holds true. To shift the dial, you have one of two choices: either build a much better sales capability (and by this we mean product, marketing, finance – everybody who contributes to the customer experience), *or* tell big whoppers about how good you are. That might just get you more sales in the short term but it's obviously a road to reputational ruin.

The big prize is in working with the customer to jointly shape the future you both want to create. If you can help the customer achieve the growth they are looking for through tailoring your product or service, you're onto a winner. It all comes down to focusing on the customer, listening to their needs and tailoring what you make to what the customer wants to buy. This, combined with building an internal team who truly believe in what they do and who have the skills and commitment to follow it through.

The feeling that the business isn't quite delivering what you want is probably the single most recurring theme we encounter in talking to directors and business owners: customers who aren't as excited about your latest innovation as you are; cautious investors (or boards) who somehow seem sceptical about the returns your new direction can offer; staff members who behave as though being employed by you is nothing more than a job.

That's not why you started out on this enterprise and it's certainly not what keeps you ticking each day. It's your heart and soul – that's why finding the customers you deserve needs you to be brutally honest. If you know in your heart of hearts that your service addresses a problem that customers need fixing, and if you know you're doing it in a way that really differentiates you, then you will find the customers you deserve.

19
Who Are My Most Important Customers?

In assessing the importance of customers, there are some simple financial measures to consider – a customer in high growth could be worth more to you in three years than a larger one in decline; a customer who costs you more in off-invoice discounts, late payment and last-minute orders is less attractive than one who's easy to deal with.

But deeper than this – and more difficult to escape – is that question of strategic alignment. If you can find a customer with whom you're on the same path; working on initiatives together; sharing benefits of cost efficiencies and exploring new markets, then that customer needs a disproportionate share of your investment and your sales team's time. It'll open doors you didn't know could open; it'll make you more profitable and it will help you sleep.

Who will be your most important customers in five years' time?

The simplest segmentation of customers is the classic four-square matrix plotting growth against attractiveness. Unsurprisingly, any customer you have in high growth and with good alignment to your business goes in the top right box. These are the customers with whom you want to overinvest, but be choosy – not all ten of the largest will fit!

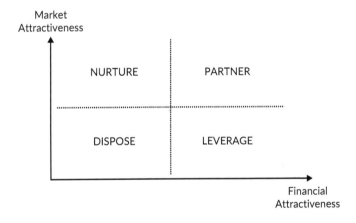

The bottom right box captures scale (they are big customers) but lacks attractiveness. Maybe it's an industry sector you don't see growing; it might be in the wrong geography or they might be partners with one of your competitors. Whatever the reason, you want to keep the (sizeable) business, but do so without overspending, so they are often referred to as cash cow customers.

The top left box is about potential and risk. At the time of planning they are not as big or as profitable as others, but you see alignment with them and getting this right can deliver high growth. Perhaps they are in a market that's about to grow and you see an opportunity to expand with them. On the other hand, they are not hugely profitable, so if growth slows, they'll no longer be attractive. Rising stars or on the decline? Only time will tell.

The bottom left box is an interesting one, as it's a box of customers you're not that bothered about. In time you might dispose of them, and it focuses the mind to think that some people you do business with might not be worth your time. If so, either radically slim down the time and energy it takes to service them or put up their prices.

This exercise of prioritising customers can be as complex or as simple as you wish. We've seen it done on a flipchart in an hour and we've seen it take a few weeks of an analyst's time, culminating in a fully bound report that segmented in detail some sixty different customers and channels. The level of detail needs to reflect the resources available and the impact the decision will make, but it's a valuable approach to adopt.

Create a customer attractiveness model

This is a two-step process. First, compile the relevant data and second, convert the data into a chart that gives you the results visually. If you've only got a small number of customers, it can be done manually but Microsoft Excel is the ideal tool.

In the data sheets you want to capture financial attractiveness (A) and market attractiveness (B) and score each out of 100. Both will be broken down into smaller parts, with each given a score.

In this example we'll keep it simple and apportion 33.3% to each criterion, but in the real world you'll probably choose to have more variables and more customers.

Step One: Data capture

Choosy Manufacturing Inc. has three customers:

1. Loyal Limited: They've been a customer as long as anybody remembers. Sales are the same every year: same products, same order size and always paid on time. Their MD plays golf with Choosy's boss.

2. Government Supplies Ltd: They buy just one product and always order more in March as the budget year comes to an end. Sales have reduced

as austerity has reduced the number of people employed. Decisions are slow as they depend on committee approval, which results in lots of sales calls. They are bad for cashflow as credit terms are tight.

3. Online Upstart Ltd (who call themselves Upst4rt): They've only traded for a couple of years but sales growth is fast. They discount online, so aggressively demand discount from you. So far, they've always paid on time through an app you've not heard of.

This is how the data sheets might appear:

A. Financial Attractiveness

Customer	Sales to customer	Margin	Cashflow
Loyal Limited	High	High	High
Govt. Supplies Ltd	Medium	Low	Low
Upst4rt	Low	Low	High

There are different considerations from a market perspective. Choosy is developing premium products and wants to connect with professionals. They also think there is opportunity to grow sales online and are keen to work with partners who have a direct-to-consumer (D2C) operation:

1. Loyal Limited: Growth potential is low. Loyal is loyal to their long-standing customers and

nervous that 'posh new products' might upset them.

2. Government Supplies Ltd: There is low growth and no real professional connection. They are big online, though.

3. Upst4rt Ltd: They plan to double their business in three years, though how isn't clear. They only target upmarket customers and most sales are online.

B. Market Attractiveness

Customer	Sales Growth	Target Consumer	Online
Loyal Limited	Low	Low	Low
Govt. Supplies Ltd	Low	Medium	High
Upst4rt	High	High	High

Step 2: Customer Attractiveness grid

In this grid we simply plot the information above, using financial and market attractiveness as the two gridlines.

For simplicity, we're awarding 25 points to a Low, 50 points to a Medium and 75 points to a High but in a real business these numbers may not be weighted equally. Then we take the average of the three.

Example: Government Supplies ranks L, M, H for the three criteria within marketing attractiveness. That's 25 + 50 + 75 = 150. Divide by 3 and the average for that criteria is 50.

This is how these three customers score in the grid:

	Financial	Market
Loyal	75	25
Govt. Supplies	33	50
Upst4rt	42	75

Placing them on a grid makes it more visual and enables us to make decisions about how we prioritise these customers:

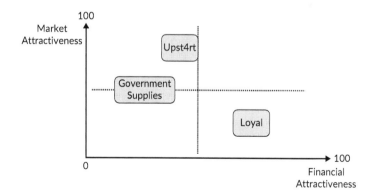

Loyal Limited is steady but unexciting. You want to keep their business as long as possible, but with the least possible investment and time. It's a classic cash cow profile.

Government Supplies is middling as a customer type and you may be able to transition them into a box that's more beneficial to you. If you could align with their online growth while improving payment terms, they could be attractive in the long term. They are a conditional growth opportunity.

Upst4rt has the most exciting potential but wouldn't pay all your bills right now. The immediate future with them is risky. With strong growth forecasts you want to stay aligned with them but would benefit from identifying opportunities together where you can innovate and grow margin.

Customer attractiveness: Act on it

From here you can begin to focus on implementing your plan in the business, making sure that any decisions and direction you've set out with are achieved. As somebody famously observed: strategy is deciding what not to do; implementation is ensuring what you agreed not to do isn't being done…

This is where pricing and investment decisions are brought to life by ensuring your team are not giving away margin and funds to your less attractive customers; where you make the tough decisions about whether your most attractive customers are the first to receive new products and services. They should be.

Answer this question wisely and you will have a team of people who know who their most important customers are. They will have the skills, tools and confidence to deal with them in subtly different ways. And you'll have the systems in place to know that your decisions are being reflected on a weekly basis in the way that customers are treated, deals are done and goods are delivered.

That's the rational stuff.

Figuring out who your most important customers are gives owners and employees a real lift. It's no longer just about having to settle for anyone who wants to do business with you even when you know that their terms will suck you dry. In moments where your pricing or value is being challenged, it replaces gut feel in helping you decide how to respond. If you've ever done it, you'll know that saying to a customer, 'Thanks, but no thanks,' can feel like a real burden lifted. It reinforces your purpose, restates your control and brings a lightness of step and a confidence in who you are.

20
How Do I Prove The Return On Investment (ROI) For This?

Many of us have learned our trade in a world where ROI is common. And simple. In the free-market economy we're so familiar with, ROI is what you get back on any given investment. It's simple to calculate and simple to assess: the incremental benefit (or return) of an investment is divided by the cost of the investment.

ROI is usually expressed as a percentage, so let's say you invest £10,000 in Google AdWords and it brings you £15,000 of sales. The simplest ROI calculation is:

$$\frac{\text{Incremental revenue £5,000}}{\text{Investment £10,000}} = \text{ROI } 50\%$$

Beware of sales tricks

Bear in mind that many businesses who are trying to sell you something will calculate the return of sales versus the investment of profit. This is misleading. To understand your business better, both sides of the calculation should be the same. In other words, if you're spending £10k of *profit* on AdWords (if you're paying an invoice you are always spending potential profit), the real ROI is measured by the amount of *profit* you deliver as a return – not the sales revenue.

What exactly you include in your measure of profit will vary by business. You could incorporate staff costs, utilities, leases and so on, but as a minimum, you should look to cover your gross profit, ie sales revenue minus cost of sales.

Let's say your business makes a gross profit of 50%. Then to truly achieve a ROI of 50% in this example, you would need extra sales of £30,000:

Incremental sales £30,000 x 50% net margin
= £15,000 net profit

$$\frac{\text{Incremental profit £5,000}}{\text{Investment £10,000}} = \text{ROI } 50\%$$

ROI calculations underpin many of the assumptions that run through Western society today. Why are bosses of big organisations given multi-million-pound bonuses? Because their bonuses are (normally) linked to the returns they generate for shareholders.

Why are nurses notoriously poorly paid, despite undertaking a day job that saves lives? For all the praise lavished on essential workers during the coronavirus outbreak, any pay increase for NHS workers will likely be kept to low single digit percentages because there is no financial ROI attached to the job they do.

In fact, many of the macro challenges we face today are in part a function of a lack of visible ROI. Why is there an obesity epidemic and an impending diabetes crisis in the UK? In part, because it's virtually impossible to look at a pack of biscuits or a bacon bap and draw the link between the immediate gratification of eating either (or both) and the risk of developing a serious disease in later life, or because you can't easily see the return on the investment of giving up your evening and going to the gym three nights a week.

Why is there a lack of affordable housing in the country? Because while we all broadly agree that families need somewhere to live, everyone invested in building – from farmers with fields designated as potential plots through to landlords, mortgage providers and major builders – are all focused on extracting a ROI from the eventual price of a house. This has pushed up the prevailing price of property to a point where fewer than 40% of adults aged twenty-five to thirty-four can afford their own homes.[24]

The world is beginning to change though, with younger generations increasingly demanding that their choice of products and services are delivered by a business with some sort of meaningful ethical credentials. The Nielsen Global Corporate Responsibility Report of 2015 showed that 73% of Millennials are prepared to spend more on a product if it comes from a sustainable brand.[25] There is a significant shift in public attitudes against the more damaging aspects of unchecked private enterprise. People are looking for business to operate to ethical standards and – increasingly – they will call out those that don't.

This raises the implication that ROI might be about more than just money and companies are changing accordingly. For example, certified B Corporations such as ourselves 'are businesses that meet the highest standards of verified social and environmental performance, public transparency, and legal accountability to balance profit and purpose.'[26] B Corp certification requires a shift in a company's articles of association to one where business owners are required to assess

---

24 'When do people buy their first home?' BBC News (31 January 2019), www.bbc.co.uk/news/business-47070020, accessed 14 January 2021

25 *The Sustainability Imperative: New insights on consumer expectations* (Nielsen, 2015), www.nielsen.com/wp-content/uploads/sites/3/2019/04/global-sustainability-report-oct-2015.pdf, accessed 24 November 2020

26 'About B Corps' (Certified B Corporation, no date), www://bcorporation.net/about-b-corps, accessed 16 November 2020

the impact of their actions not just on shareholders, but on employees, communities and the environment.

It is rarely what corporations want us to believe – and advertising and PR is designed to direct attention away from this simple truth – but their primary purpose is to make money for their shareholders. It's written in their articles of association. It's the law. Remember this next time you view a TV advert showing a cute puppy pulling toilet roll or a perfectly curated family skipping through a field in their whiter-than-white leisure wear.

What's the 'return' in ROI?

How many times do you get to the end of something and utter the words, 'I wish I hadn't bothered'? It might be an underwhelming dinner at a posh restaurant you've been looking forward to for months. It might be doing someone a favour that wasn't received as positively as you'd expected. More likely it's a tough business project that ate up your time and energy only to fall short of expectations.

With ROI so prevalent, business owners have many choices about what they want ROI to mean for them. We like the B Corp model because it retains the profit motive for shareholders, which we believe drives innovation and efficiency, but it ensures that this is balanced with other outcomes.

Alternatively, some organisations exist solely to achieve a societal end. There are 'not for profits' that make it their goal to help rehabilitate ex-offenders, to employ those with mental health problems or to smooth the path of ex-servicemen and women back into the workplace. Founders can take a salary, but they'll never be able to sell to a trade investor and make a million.

What this demonstrates is that ROI is much more than a simple calculation. It's a strategic choice about the type of organisation you choose to run, which in turn will influence the type of people you choose to recruit and the type of people who opt to join you.

ROI and people

There is growing evidence that businesses with a clear purpose – and it's certainly true for B Corps – find that it helps them recruit the talent that they need to achieve their commercial aims. The connection between ROI and people isn't just about whether your sales team are giving you the numbers you need to meet budget. There's a much broader consideration about the communities you recruit your people from and the role you play in developing those localities.

At a more functional level, it's also worth considering how flexible you can be with people. It's surprising how fixated many businesses still are on the full-time, permanent route for filling a position. In larger organisations this may be a result of the process necessary to have headcount added to the budget. Once you've navigated this procedure it's difficult to explain why you want a part-timer.

Smaller businesses have no such excuse. For example, many organisations transition from no sales director to sales director in a short space of time. It's not just sales, of course, but given our line of work that's one we see relatively frequently. That rarely makes sense. For a growing business, the day they are sizeable enough to need a sales director is a great milestone of success – sales are growing and customers are spending more – but that growth is generally organic. It's more sensible to move from no sales director to having someone on board for maybe a day or two a week. If someone is needed daily, then five half-days might suit. Continued success then leads to an increase in the number of days over time.

There's a massive body of talent across the world – weighted towards women – that would be more engaged in the world of work if flexible working was an option. It's not just grandstanding. Research by respected institutions such as the United Nations repeatedly shows that encouraging greater workplace diversity and adopting flexible working practices is good for economic growth.[27] Why miss out?

---

27 'Gender Equality' (UN, no date), www.un.org/en/sections/issues-depth/gender-equality, accessed 14 January 2021

Cashflow and ROI

One of the factors to consider in connection with ROI is the importance of cashflow. Cash is king. It's not so much a return on investment; more a return on activity. You need confidence that the return will come. If you still want to invest that £10,000 in AdWords you not only need to know what the ROI is, you need to know when you'll get the money.

If leads are converted in the month after the ads are placed, you invoice the month after that and half your customers pay a few days late, you could be waiting three months for the return. Get excited and run the same campaign every month and you will have spent £30,000 on Google before you've received a penny. In the meantime, you've probably paid your raw material suppliers to their strict terms, so you're out of pocket both ways.

It's worse as you grow, of course. Double the spend each month because 'we're generating loads of leads' and the cash crisis bites more quickly and more deeply. It can quickly become uncomfortable indeed.

Customer lifetime value

A second measure that's helpful in connection with ROI is thinking about Customer Lifetime Value (CLV). It flows neatly from discussion about AdWords.

Say your AdWords spend generates an average first order of £500. Each one of those new customers might cost you a couple of hundred pounds in advertising, on top of which you have to go through your whole selling process, send out quotes and carry out credit checks. Plus, there's the basic cost of your service, whether that's a product you're creating and shipping, or the labour cost of providing a service. Maybe both.

It's not unusual for the first order from a customer to be little better than breakeven for the selling business.

Let's say your cost of goods is 50% – in this example that's £250 – with the cost of selling, processing and shipping the order adding another £80, on top of your AdWords spend of £200. After all that investment and activity, the net profit from all this energy is –£30.

The prize is in what happens next.

When that same customer orders the following year, you already have them set up in your CRM system. You've done the credit check and they understand how you send out quotes. They were happy with the first order so the next quote can be short and quick.

As they're confident in you, the second order comes in at £800. Because the admin's complete and you've not paid AdWords this time, profit is a whopping £400.

Don't you love a happy customer? Work out how long a customer stays with you and you can establish the CLV. If you're in an industry where loyalty is strong you might find customers stay for, say, five years or more.

In this example you would generate £1,570 of net profit from that first investment of £200 in AdWords (−£30 in year one, followed by 4 x years at £400).

Customer Lifetime Value (CLV)	Year 1 Order	Year 2 Order	Next 3 Years' Orders
Value of Order	£500	£800	£2,400
Cost of Goods	£250	£400	£1,200
Cost of New Customer	£280	£0	£0
Net Profit	−£30	£400	£1,200

This is at the heart of the promotion strategies of many industries. Take, for example, CRM systems, which most small business owners will be all too familiar with. All CRM providers offer a 'first month free' deal during which you can test out their system and assess its capabilities. More important, they can smother you with service calls and welcome emails so that you decide to stick with them post-trial. Why? Because they are fixated on CLV.

How much hassle is it to load all your contact details into a new CRM system and create all those bespoke reports that tell you how you're performing? Do you really have the patience to pick through the remnants of your old CRM system (so last year, darling) to find emails from important clients? No. CRM companies know that it's worth the free month's trial (cost to them – zero) and the over-enthusiastic sales calls and tutorials (cost to them – maybe £100) because you'll stay for life and diligently pay them each month. Even if you've subscribed for just £10 per month, that's £1,200 over a decade; before inflation-busting price increases. Worth every penny of the £100 of support you receive in month one. That's the beauty of CLV.

The accumulator bet with CLV is the value of referrals. If your customer is happy with the service they receive in the first few months, not only do you benefit from the repeat revenue they spend, but they are also likely to recommend you to others. That honeymoon period is the best time to ask for referrals and reviews. Referrals and word of mouth are such powerful influences that this can multiply the CLV from a specific customer. In certain industries it's worth identifying those who you'd designate as your advocates and giving them special treatment. Think of CRM companies who are always happy to offer you a free month (cost to them, still zero) if you refer a colleague.

The ROI on ROI

ROI is a simple calculation, but one that affects strategic decisions and company direction. It affects the type of people you attract and retain, and it impacts on tactical decisions, day-to-day plans and policies. This puts it firmly and squarely at the centre of a company's success in selling.

When ROI falls into place for a business we see a real sense of calm come over the team running the company. Gone are those scary days when investment decisions were all a bit seat-of-the-pants; when even as you pressed the button you knew it might end up as a 'wishing I'd not bothered' experience. In its place is an opportunity for a grown-up group of leaders to carry the authority of knowing where they are heading, what they're trying to do and what ROI they'll use to measure success.

21

Can You Help Me Become Confident In Sales?

Confidence in sales is about two complementary things: belief in yourself and what you're selling, and the technical skill necessary to do this well and coach others to do the same.

Let's explore the confidence aspect first. Is it possible to be afraid of sales? We're not talking about spiders, tall buildings or Justin with the cleaver at the local butchery counter. We're talking about the fear of rejection. For many people this gets to the heart of Sales Myth #11: I Can't Sell. Natural born hunters don't know this feeling exists. Somebody slamming a door in their face is simply the prelude to the next opportunity, but for most of us – and we count ourselves here – rejection is painful. If you've spent three years locked in a laboratory developing the world's best organic shampoo only for Boots or Superdrug to tell you it doesn't deserve a place on their shelves, then that hurts. It's personal. The way to overcome this is to establish distance between yourself and the product. If the buyer thinks your product is too mainstream, too expensive or too green, then accept that as feedback. Feedback can help the next stage of development of your product, but remind yourself daily that it's not a rejection of you.

What role best suits you?

What you want to achieve is probably about generating revenue or achieving growth, so go back to the hunter/farmer debate and ask yourself what type of sales approach your business needs. Are you looking for someone who can knock on one door after another to open new revenue streams or do you need someone reliable and trustworthy who can build relationships with existing customers and be relied on to deliver promises?

Which of those roles best describes you? From today, focus on getting better at the role you can do and recognise that either now or later you'll need to hire someone to do the other job. Running a business is supposed to be liberating, so don't get hung up on trying to be something you're not. There's much evidence in management training circles to demonstrate that you're best off training someone in what they are best at. Yes, you can train to improve weaknesses, but unless you have a dangerous weakness in one area the biggest return is achieved by becoming brilliant at what you enjoy and have a talent for. In today's world this has the added benefit of ticking the authenticity box. Customers and clients expect you to be honest and most professional buyers are pretty good at working out what strengths suppliers have and finding ways of accommodating them.

There are a couple of pointers here:

Firstly, please don't think you have to be pushy or extrovert to be able to sell. Of course, you need to be determined enough to seek out opportunities to place your product or service in front of decision-makers – doors don't open without being pushed – but a good sales person has two ears and one mouth. Use them in that proportion. The time-worn perception that sales people are smooth talkers isn't always true and increasingly might not wash with a sceptical public. If you find yourself in a car showroom or a bank, would you sooner have someone who prattles on about their favourite car or the best insurance policy or would you feel more comfortable with someone who explores you? What you need, what you want it for, how you intend to use it. Time and again we come across sales teams where money is left on the table because they've not explored the client's full needs and only walked out with an order for part of what the client wanted. Asking and listening are truly undervalued skills in sales.

The second pointer is passion. This should be second nature if you're the founder of a business and have spent many years developing a product or service to the point where it's properly saleable, but as employees it's equally impactful on a sceptical buyer. You might not have a certificate from the Procter & Gamble training academy on your wall, but if you care passionately about what you're selling it's infectious. This is when it's important to remember the two ears, one mouth advice. Enthusiasm will take you a long way and can encourage decision-makers to be surprisingly accommodating, but they still want to believe you've taken the time to explore whether your world-beating product is right for them and will meet their needs.

The technical aspect

What some people mean by 'I can't sell' is that they don't feel confident in recruiting or managing sales people – without the benefit of a training manual they don't know what the mechanics of selling look like. There are a couple of tools that can be useful here.

Structuring a sales conversation

Those of us growing up in major consumer businesses had the steps of the call drummed into us. Each business had its own version: the '9 x 6' or the '7 x 5'. As a sales manager your daily job was to accompany a sales rep and coach them in this structure. We had this approach drilled into us in an era of Ford Mondeos and Oasis, but the discipline of most of these steps still holds true in sales conversations today. The crucial thing about these approaches is that the sales pitch only comes in the second half of the process. Imagine your sales person is selling vegetarian food to independent food stores. The flow you create for the call would look something like this:

Step	Purpose	Detail
1	Plan	Review previous conversation and set objectives for today's call.
2	Prepare	Make sure you have the latest promotion offers and samples of new product packaging to show.
3	Pre-call	Assess what's happening in the neighbourhood. New housing developments, competitors running promotions and so on. What promotion themes are given space at the front of store or promoted in the window?
4	Introduction	Greet the owner and tell them you'd like to have a look around first. Resist the temptation to sell.

Continued

Cont.

Step	Purpose	Detail
5	Store check	Have a look around the store, noting major price and promotion activity. See what level of stock the store is holding of your and your competitor's products. This will affect order size. Remove any of your stock that's damaged.
6	Real selling	At last: now you can get to the reason for visiting, but instead of just flogging your latest range and special offers you're prepared to have a conversation about what's selling well (low stock levels), how vegan food is selling (you noticed the poster in the window) and how customer numbers are improving (the new block of flats around the corner). It's not just a hard sell – it's you demonstrating knowledge and insight.

(Oh, and you've kindly replaced a couple of boxes that were damaged – not your obligation, but the price of samples is low and favours are always appreciated...) |
| 7 | Take the order | Who could resist a conversational proposal like yours? |
| 8 | Merchandising | Before leaving the store, you check the store room and ensure all your product slots are filled with stock and shelving is neat and tidy. |

Continued

Cont.

Step	Purpose	Detail
9	Post-call admin	You record the conversation, put the order into the system and make a note of what you picked up about the customer.
		Crucially, you provisionally annotate what your objectives might be for the next call. The buyer did mention that the competitor's vegan line was selling slowly...

You can capture this sort of process on a page. It will not turn an amateur into a professional but it provides a structure that helps address the 'I can't sell' challenge. When you do bring in new sales people it's a benchmark for sales conversations that instils that winning confidence within the team.

This retail structure adapts easily to other sectors. Let's say you're making outbound calls selling customer management software to a university. The neighbourhood is how they are promoting themselves on social media and your competitor check is done online. Turning up to a sales conversation able to show you've checked their website, reviewed the customer journey and are aware of your competitor's 'hilarious' YouTube video (yawn) shows you've made the effort to provide them with insight beyond the sales pitch. You can't exactly do a store check, but you can keep up to date with industry newsfeeds for their sector and hold a meaningful conversation about how their competitor's new website is performing.

Telesales call benchmarking

When working with telesales (or internal sales) people making outbound calls, you can use an assessment tool for each step of the call. Again, it's a means of structuring the key activities of the call with standards captured for each. There will be some high-level steps, such as Intro, Call and Close, on top of which you might assess interpersonal skills or negotiation skills. Each of these is broken into component steps, so Call might include:

- Identify client need

- Act on buying signals

- Confirm client need

- Sell your company benefits

- Identify the decision-maker

- Ask about cross-sell opportunities

An extract from the completed template might look like this:

Key element	Good practice	Current practice	Quotes/ examples of best practice
Call			
Identify client need			
Act on buying signals	Able to recognise buying signals and respond to cues from client eg, 'It's urgent,' or, 'I've been let down.'	When mentioned by client these are responded to, but the team don't ask probing questions to explore.	'I really need this as fast as you can,' to be picked up by sales person and rapid delivery agreed.
Confirm client need			
Sell your company's benefits			
Identify the decision-maker			
Ask about cross-sell opportunities			

Before you listen to 100 telesales calls and create a weighty body of evidence, it is worth asking, 'What does this mean?' What will you do with this when it's complete? Will you have the time, patience and coaching skills to ensure your team will buy into the results and be keen to learn? If so, then it will provide an immensely useful assessment of how well your team are performing at present and what you can do to improve it.

Business leaders who can demonstrate confidence in selling radiate such positivity that it's worth investing time and resources in this. There's an infectious positivity that flows from the boss being able to describe the aspects of sales (or finance, or marketing) that they can do and the elements they have learned or figured out along the way.

In truth, few employees expect you to be perfect. Having the humility to explain that you've never been professionally trained in sales but have achieved measurable progress by applying yourself can be a highly motivational message – for them and for you.

22

How Do I Choose Between Hunters And Farmers?

There are many models describing different types of sales people. If you were to adopt just one, then the simplicity of the hunter/farmer is the one we suggest.

This model states that there are essentially two types of sales people: hunters are driven to build connections, strike deals and win the business. In contrast, farmers (sometimes called nurturers) are great at building long-term partnerships and finding ways of evolving relationships over time. Once the deal is complete, give a hunter six months of looking after that same client and they'll be bored. On the other hand, a farmer won't find the adrenaline of winning the deal to be enough: reward comes more from the loyalty and sustainability of client relationships.

Like all simple interpretations of personality, the health warning that comes with this is that humans tend not to sit at the extreme of either axis, but crucially, the vast majority of sales people will not have high capability on both dimensions. This means that identifying the primary personality you need for any given role is essential to your future success.

Hunter Ingredients	Farmer Ingredients
Enjoy the pursuit of new business: great at acquisition	Enjoy long-term relationships: great at retention
Proactive networkers and strong influencers	Strong service ethic and sense of loyalty
Highly resilient in the face of resistance and take 'No' as an opportunity	Concerned that 'No' means letting people down and being unreliable
Independent operators who work at pace	Team players whose conscientious approach can result in a heavy workload
Focus on closing the deal	Focus on nurturing the relationship
Need high financial rewards for personal performance	Need emotional rewards for personal growth
Likely to change jobs frequently	Likely to be loyal employees

Sales people are pre-programmed to favour one of these approaches – it's in the DNA. If you think back over your previous sales experiences you probably have a hunch about where you sit on the scale. If you're the type who attends lots of events, returning to the office with lots of warm leads, the type who goes out for lunch and returns with a new client, then your natural tendency is likely to be that of hunter. If you don't find that approach feels natural, then you're more likely a farmer. Neither is better or worse, but selecting the right one for your job is critical.

Has social media changed this model?

Social selling is moving so quickly that this is a constantly evolving picture. Still, there's no reason to believe that a sales person's underlying personality type has changed because of the proliferation of online sales opportunities, so the hunter/farmer distinction still holds true.

The way you hunt can be different though. It's now possible to play the numbers game of reaching out to new prospects by utilising the right algorithms on LinkedIn. There are various tools that can automate the whole system, so in many industries the job description of hunter doesn't look like it used to.

Our take on this is that there is a third role emerging that sits somewhere between hunter and farmer: the fisher. It's more proactive than a traditional farmer but more nuanced than an old-school hunter. The fisher puts out the right sort of bait in the form of online connections and content marketing and jiggles them around in a way that encourages bites. An extreme hunter might find this boring while an extreme farmer would still feel uncomfortable with how pushy this feels.

This hybrid means that organisationally it might be as much a marketing job as a sales role, but the hunter/ farmer principle will still apply. A hunter in this job will be driven by a high number of outreach messages and unshaken by numerous negative responses. A farmer will seek to engage in a smaller number of relationships and conversations. Your recruitment choice should still be driven by the job you need doing.

What if I only have one sales position?

In small businesses it might just be the owner who does the selling, or maybe there's only one other sales person. The role is inevitably a jack-of-all-trades. In this case the hunter/farmer principle remains, and you'll still find the best fit by identifying what the primary role for the job will be.

If you can subsequently shape the role to fit the incumbent, you'll be happier with results. If, for example, you recruit a hunter, can you find someone else who is happy to farm back in the office? Perhaps you can create part-time roles or outsource certain tasks to ensure people spend as much of their time as possible on where they have the biggest impact.

Why can't someone be both hunter and farmer?

The hunter/farmer axis is driven by underlying preference and as most people end up doing what they are good at it's rare to find someone equally skilled in both. One way of viewing this is to look at the make-up of a cricket team. Every national team has batters, bowlers and probably one all-rounder. In these teams you'll find a batter who can bowl a bit and a bowler who's good for a few runs. Skills can be learned and having an underlying preference doesn't render you useless at the other role, but the team's designated all-rounder is never the number one either at batting or bowling.

If you apply this thinking back in the workplace it's clear you can get a job done with an all-rounder, but if you have the budget you'll score faster and take more wickets by having the right personality in the right job.

What do you want to achieve?

Every sales and marketing activity you undertake as a business owner should have a Call to Action attached to it. It's the 'What does this mean?' again: who is your message aimed at and what do you want them to do differently?

Deciding whether you want hunters or farmers is dependent first and foremost on the quality of your plan. What do you want to achieve? Business owners often present us with a conundrum such as, 'I just need to improve my conversion rates,' or, 'My sales team aren't making outbound calls,' or, 'Nobody is calling lapsed customers.'

The nub of this issue is that you've probably not recruited hunters to make those outbound calls. Your existing customers could be well-looked after, enjoying positive personal relationships with your team. Some months they might pay on time and your sales are consistently growing but that doesn't make your sales team any more than farming order processors. If you really need to be making outbound calls and persuading customers that you're the number one supplier for them, then you need hunters. You can have both, just not in the same brain.

One reason this is such a prevalent issue is that the business world according to Google is seemingly full of consultants and advisors who advocate a narrow focus on the sales funnel. Their compelling narrative, which is usually accompanied by testimonials about businesses that 'doubled their profits in ten weeks using these five magic steps' and supported by *shouty language that makes you buy,* suggests that a simple fix to the sales funnel will transform your business. It won't, but that's all they sell.

Our advice is to not spend a penny until you're clear what you want to spend it on. This really is one of those areas where a plan is vital in ensuring you spend your money once and spend it wisely. Nor does it matter whether you're spending on marketing messages (website, email, social media…) or head-count – the principle is the same.

What does my customer need?

A great way of looking at this is to take your sales funnel and turn it inside out to think about what customers experience at each phase of their life stage with your business. Few customers would use this thinking or vocabulary to describe their interaction with you, but what matters is that you understand the decision your customer is about to reach and make that choice as simple for them as possible. Be easy to do business with.

This assessment will take customers from a point before they've even heard of you, right through to the place where you're looking in the rear-view mirror and reflecting on what they were like to do business with. So for every stage in that journey you can iden-tify what action you want them to take to continue their journey with you rather than your competitors. Then you can ensure people with the appropriate skills and mindset for that stage are the ones doing the jobs.

Hunters or farmers? This alignment of planning and people is another reason to value this simple model.

Making an important appointment to your team usually brings a sense of excitement, for you and the individual. Have you noticed how the right new joiner transforms your business within the first month? The excitement bubbles and now it's not just you and the HR manager who ran the recruitment that are noticing. Others are catching the bug and the whole team has had a lift – powerful stuff.

Right person, right job.

23
How Do I Recruit Great Sales People?

'So, thanks for coming in. Why don't you take me through your CV?'

'So, thanks for coming in. Why don't you have a go at riding this unicorn?'

Only one of these sentences has any obvious link to recruiting a person into your business, unless you have a specific need for a unicorn rider and know where the unicorns are parked. Maybe one appears more fanciful than the other. In fact, both are about as useless as each other when it comes to finding and assessing a person's likely fit and capability within your business, but one continues to be used repeatedly as the start of what appears to be a rigorous and fair process. One that often leads to disappointment, wasted time and money. And there are never any unicorns.

Corporate businesses have whole teams of people dedicated to ensuring that their recruitment processes are effective and fair, although in the age of instant CV uploads which allow candidates to apply for 100 jobs in an afternoon, personalised interaction has mainly been sacrificed for automated rejection emails, speed and efficiency.

Many large organisations deliberately anonymise CVs and deploy algorithms to filter potential candidates with the aim of disregarding gender, race, age and other irrelevant markers that a name or personal information may signpost. They'll also filter applicants via online and virtual tests long before any of them find themselves in front of a human who may smile at them.

All of this becomes much more of a challenge when it's your own business and you're the one writing the job advert, screening the applications (or cajoling the agency you've employed into doing it thoroughly for you) and interviewing people. You know this could transform your business. You also understand that getting it wrong will cost time and money and could have significant ramifications across your business for all involved. So where to start? There are three key stages to get this right: planning to recruit, filtering CVs and the interview process itself.

Planning to recruit

This is the stage most often overlooked and most crucial to what happens next. On a busy Monday when you're balancing 101 other urgent tasks it might be tempting to quickly edit an old advert and pop it straight onto a job board or LinkedIn with no further thought, happy in the knowledge it's one less thing to worry about, but the lack of worrying at this stage will cause endless worrying later in the process. Better to afford yourself some time to think about and plan exactly who and exactly what you are looking for before you hit the upload button.

Creating the job specification

Is there a current and relevant job description? If it's an existing sales role in your business, does the job description truly reflect what's being done by the person in the role now or does it need updating to reflect reality? If it's a brand-new role, what are the key components?

What type of selling are you expecting? Inbound calls and upselling? Making outbound calls to prospective new clients? Or will the person be managing relationships and cross-selling to existing clients? What else about your business do you want to share with applicants? What are your values, what makes you different, unusual and attractive to work for?

Here is an example of a basic job description template:

Job Title	Sales Development Manager
Reports to	Sales Director
Date and Version	v1. January 2021

Aim of Role (maximum of three aims):

Contribute towards our target of increasing revenue, profit and market share by delivering new business sales within the industry.

Etc

Duties, including but not limited to... (maximum of seven duties):

Lead conversion. Your leads will come from telemarketing, direct mail and inbound inquiries driven by our marketing team. You will prioritise your interactions ensuring that all suspects and prospects are qualified according to the agreed sales process and visible via the CRM system.

Etc

Authority and Key Measures:

Can make commercial decisions on designated customers excluding changes to list price.

Measures:

- Deliver sales target of £250k in Year 1.
- Customer satisfaction.

Etc

Continued

Cont.

Skills/Qualifications:

- Business development. Proven ability to identify sales opportunities, nurture prospects and deliver sales results.
- Sales funnel management. Able to qualify prospects and accurately forecast current and future month sales to the business.
- Organisational skills. Able to prioritise workload of yourself and others and co-ordinate teams across different internal and external functions.

Etc

What exactly are you looking for in a candidate?

This simple template can be a useful tool to assist your thinking. The notes column is where you begin to define the style and approach of the person you're really looking for.

Planning to recruit	Notes
If you're replacing a person who's leaving you, what have you learned from having them in your business regarding what you need in the next person who joins you?	
Are you willing to grow your own talent (a person with potential) or do you need someone already operating at this level?	
Is there a core skill missing within your existing team that this new person needs to bring?	

Continued

Cont.

Planning to recruit	Notes
What *must* the new person have in terms of expertise, professional certification, knowledge, attitude, values and skills?	
What are you willing or able to develop in them once they arrive?	
What are the red flags in terms of attitude or behaviours that you want to avoid bringing into your business?	
Is this full-time, part-time or could the role be shared? How flexible are you willing to be to find the right person/people?	

What about your business (and you)?

What first impression do you want to create with your advert and how will you make it distinct and engaging? What's the best way for applicants to respond to your advert? You could ask them to simply submit a CV or complete an application or test or you might ask them to call you for a conversation (a great way to identify candidates who are proactive if you need that).

Given the attributes you've identified above, decide where you are most likely to find candidates that match – via agencies, LinkedIn, local networking, Mumsnet, Facebook, etc. Only once you're certain that you understand the 'who you are looking for' and the 'what they'll be doing' should you author an advert.

And that's just the beginning.

Filtering CVs

You've decided on the type of candidate you're looking for. You know the level of experience and skill versus cultural and behavioural fit you're searching for. How do you shortlist from the 100 CVs that descend into your inbox?

The world is now increasingly aware of the risk of litigation from unsuccessful applicants. It could relate to a claim of unfairness in the process or a lack of transparency in how decisions and assessments are made. Whether the actual decisions were fair or unfair is often a moot point as it's the lack of demonstrable rigour and recording of how the assessment was made that undermines the entire process. A claim made against you here will cost you far more than the time taken to ensure your process is as fair and transparent as possible. Gut feel never survives contact with employment law.

It can be useful to have a predetermined set of criteria and a scoring mechanism with which to assess each CV. These will vary between businesses but here's a simple list that captures some of the common considerations. The ideal way of completing this is to use a colour-coded traffic light system in a Microsoft Word table: green means great, just what you're looking for; red is a big watch-out; amber an unproven. With lots of CVs this will give you a straightforward, visual way of filtering out the hot candidates:

	Candidate A	Candidate B	Candidate C
Are there anomalies in the CV, such as unexplained gaps between jobs?			
Are the CV and covering letter grammatically correct and has care been taken in how they're presented?			
Does the CV highlight achievements and results within the jobs performed or just list activities and tasks carried out?			
Has the CV been tailored for this specific application or is it just a generalised version that appears to be used for any role?			
Are there jobs within the CV where the candidate has joined and left within a short space of time?			
Does the CV demonstrate advancement or just job-hopping between similar roles in different organisations?			
Do the candidate's education, work-based training and/or qualifications demonstrate an ability to learn and develop?			
Do their hobbies suggest an ability to learn and grow?			
Does the candidate have previous experience of this role, or would it be brand new to them (either as promotion or a sidestep)?			
Does the candidate possess the job-critical skills, knowledge and attributes you'd expect from the jobs listed within their CV?			

After this filtering, the final question that requires an honest answer before you commit to any interviews is this. Is the CV truly appealing and relevant for the role or is it just the best of a bad bunch? If so, is this good enough for you and your business? Bums on seats is rarely a basis for successful recruitment.

Conducting the interview

When the day arrives and it's time to interview your candidates it can be tempting to rely on a mix of gut feel, a few random questions and a hope that at least one candidate turns up on time and looks interested, but you'll be doing yourself and your business a disservice. The attributes you've identified as being important should shape your interview process.

If you're still to be convinced of the importance of a structured interview or have been lucky to acquire great calibre people thus far, then here's some further food for thought. Schmidt and Hunter performed meta-analysis of eighty-five years of research evaluating how well assessments predict the future performance of candidates. They discovered that structured interviews are 34% more effective at predicting performance than unstructured.[28] The candidate's age, years

---

28 FL Schmidt and JE Hunter, 'The validity and utility of selection methods in personnel psychology: Practical and theoretical implications of 85 years of research findings', *Psychological Bulletin*, 124: 2 (1998), pp262–274, https://doi.org/10.1037/0033-2909.124.2.262, accessed 14 January 2021

of education and biographical data have almost zero correlation with their future success. That's mostly the stuff that CVs present with such aplomb.

Competency-based questions test the level to which skills can be applied consistently and can help differentiate between candidates who have developed experience and skills. Behavioural-based questions help seek out behaviours from candidates that may not have the exact experience or skills you need, but who could adapt and learn. Useful for the 'grow your own' option.

The thinking you've done before placing the advert should point you in the direction of which is more appropriate – most likely a mix of both. The types of questions you ask should be shaped around these. For example, influence and persuasiveness are likely key to success in a sales role. You might define this as: use flexible interpersonal styles to convince others of your point of view and gain commitment to a plan or idea.

You may want to ask questions such as:

- Describe a situation where you were able to influence others on an important issue. What approaches or strategies did you use?

- Tell me about an idea or initiative that you sold to your line manager which represented a challenge.

- Tell me about a time when you overcame a serious objection from a client. What did you do and why?

Having a transparent and objective scoring mechanism against which to assess answers helps ensure you're able to compare everyone fairly (assuming of course you've written the answers down and not been seduced by a story involving a saddle and a horse with a twisted magical horn).

Attributes Required (R) / Desired (D)	Candidate A Evidence	Candidate B Evidence	Candidate C Evidence
Influence and persuasiveness (R)			
Results orientation (R)			
Team working (R)			
Proactivity (D)			
Customer service orientation (R)			
Applied knowledge of Application XXT.13Rs (D)			
Expertise in KAMdot.expert (R)			

Continued

Cont.

Attributes Required (R) / Desired (D)	Candidate A Evidence	Candidate B Evidence	Candidate C Evidence
Values aligned to our business: Honesty, co-operation and 'customer first'			
Assessment of candidate suitability			
Decision			

It's normal to have copious pages of notes from an interview and if this isn't your skill it can be useful to have a second interviewer to capture all that's said. Nor do you have to rely just on questions – it's perfectly reasonable to test a candidate's ability to do what they say they can, provided what they are asked to do is close to the real-life tasks they are being interviewed for.

We once recruited for a marketing position with a client. The job needed someone who could check the on-pack copy for healthcare products and who could write and post on social media so we specified that candidates must be able to write accurate copy. At interview we gave everyone a simple test that involved writing a short report. No phones, no laptop, no spell-check. From a shortlist of five, we rejected two candidates based on this test. Their interviews were fine, and they would have stayed in the process were it not for the extra effort. Time well spent. It might extend your interview process to ninety minutes instead of an hour, but testing people on must-have skills will give you more observable and reliable data than any jog through a CV.

And back to you again

It's an investment of your and others' time to get recruitment right. Of course, there's no such thing as absolute certainty, but as with any investment you make for your business, wouldn't you prefer to be sure that you've done all you can to ensure your investment pays off? How reassured would you feel knowing that more than just intuition had helped determine someone's suitability for a crucial role in your business?

The broader consideration with recruitment is how it's a part of your brand. How you communicate with applicants and even how you let them down gives a message to your community about what it's really like to work for you. That's why Glassdoor exists. How you say 'No, thank you' to an initial application or a candidate you've interviewed will have as much bearing on your reputation as the actual appointment you make.

If you really receive 100 applications, the painful truth is you'll reject ninety-nine. For the sake of a little time to automate a kindly, 'Thank you for your interest in us and we wish you well with your job search,' your business will still stand head and shoulders above the hundreds of organisations who think nothing of ignoring all but the last three candidates they wish to interview.

Likewise, how you communicate with candidates still in the process is key. Priorities change, managers go on holiday and unpredictable things derail the business: being honest and open with candidates during these periods does so much to engender enthusiasm and trust and it pays back in the long run. The fact you've acknowledged candidates as human beings and treated them with courtesy will have created people who think and speak more positively about your business to others.

24

How Do I Get The Best Out Of New Sales People?

Bringing new sales people on board is a mix of strategy and emotion. There's the planning and rational thinking that you need to identify the right type of person and then ensure your new recruit is the round peg you think you've interviewed. Once you've asked someone to change the company they work for, the journey they take to work and the skills they're developing, there's also a moral imperative to help them deliver their best for you. Aside from that, it's just good business.

PLAN FOR SUCCESS

Henri had a new sales person joining his team. Her advance publicity was amazing. Before she'd even stepped foot in the business, everyone had heard all about her successes elsewhere: the doubling of her client list, the over-achievement of targets, the skills she brought to closing deals. What a difference she was going to make. Hurrah!

Henri knew from bitter experience that unless he ensured she joined the business supported by an effective onboarding process, all this PR would be to no avail and might even set her up to fail. What a waste. It had happened to him before and he was determined to do things differently now that he had the chance.

His onboarding had been nonexistent. Everyone had been friendly and welcoming, but he'd had no formal induction at all. He'd discovered later that everyone had been distracted by the potential of a new client being won. That had been followed by a rush to close sales before quarter end, sorting out problems with the temperamental server and then a crucial delivery getting lost. With one thing and another, his onboarding had never quite made it to the top of anyone's list.

He'd joined the team in a flurry of busyness, and after four weeks of people taking it in turns to answer his questions, there was tacit agreement that he understood what he was doing and was happily getting on with it. No one had realised how close Henri had come to leaving, when he began to doubt his decision and his abilities and wonder whether the business cared.

That had been eighteen months ago, and Henri estimated that for at least seven of those months he'd been working out what was expected of him, learning how the business actually worked and trying to do the right thing – not the easiest way to make a difference.

So, in spite of having a team to lead, customers to care for and a supply problem to resolve, Henri switched off his email and dedicated time to ensuring his new recruit was given the best possible chance of succeeding when she joined his team.

Make a good start

Onboarding new hires properly takes a sound plan, time and energy. Painfully, it means new people won't be chasing customers as quickly as you'd hoped, but consider the alternative. What does it say to your existing team when new hires are baffled by acronyms, unsure of product details and can't find the nearest sandwich bar? Worse, what does it say to your customers when your representative is smart, smiley and uninformed?

Yes, a thorough induction can mean additional days before your new recruit starts to deliver, but it's an investment that will pay back with them, with their colleagues and with your customers. Underlying the propensity of businesses to overlook the importance of induction is a misunderstanding of the costs of selling.

Small business can't always match the onboarding sophistication of corporate business when new people join – there simply isn't the process and structure. Phew. What small businesses can do brilliantly is care.

Everything is personal. Translating this into the way in which a new starter is integrated can be enhanced by a few simple actions. Not all of these will work in your organisation but try it as a checklist and see how many you can tick off.

Ten ways to excite new joiners

1. **Stay in touch before the big day.** Make them feel wanted and included (but not drowned in data and tedious company 'stuff'). Ensure they know the basics like dress code, how people get lunch and where to park.

2. **Form a welcoming committee.** Ensure that your existing team is ready for them joining you. Your people want to know who is joining, the role they'll be doing, where they fit in and a bit about their background. Organise a day one coffee and cake meeting or a lunch and invite everyone. Cake – any excuse.

3. **Create a plan for day one in advance.** Beyond the practicalities like computer passwords and phone, can you make their day special with a welcome pack? Make sure you've thought about their learning and development plan and their manager is clear on what support they need.

4. **Lead the celebration.** Do everything you can to welcome them personally. In huge corporates new starters don't expect to meet their CEO or MD

on day one (or even month one). Expectations are different in smaller businesses. You being there and caring about how they join is a really important first impression.

5. **Connect people.** A team coffee or biscuit break is enough, even if it's virtual. Ensuring people quickly establish social relationships with others in your business is really important. It helps reduce anxiety and the sensation of being an outsider and increases the speed with which they commit to your business and feel part of it.

6. **Provide a buddy or a mentor.** This provides enormous value in helping the person become knowledgeable quickly and can also help them navigate the quirks in your business that aren't written down anywhere but make a real difference to how life works out. You might not know that your team have learned not to ask you anything difficult before you've drunk your first cup of caffeine-rich Costa Rican coffee, but they do, and they'll tell the new starter.

7. **Help them grow and make it fun.** Create a learning plan with them that's tailored to them. Avoid at all costs the feeling or actuality of their being sheep-dipped through an out-of-date series of slides or experiences. Agree learning objectives and outcomes and ensure they own them. Spend time explaining the talent and promise you saw in them and how that fits within the business. Share your expectations of them and ask what theirs are

of you. Identify the areas they are going to focus on in developing their skills further. This sets a really important expectation that you'll act, so ensure you follow up. You captured all this in the interview notes described in the last chapter.

8. **Make it interactive.** Do everything you can to create an experience that is multi-sensory, technologically varied, participative and interactive. Abandoning someone with PowerPoint presentations does not make a learning environment. Making them watch others present is a recipe for an early exit. Be consistent. Commit to meet regularly with your new starter over the first six months. Coach them (learn how to, if this isn't your natural style) and encourage curiosity, feedback and observation – from all involved.

9. **Give them real work.** Watching a newly learned skill or process being used in real time is of much greater value than asking a person either to confirm they know how to do something or to just verbally describe the theory of it. This is less about kicking them out the door with a sales presentation and more about making them actively involved in real activity at an early stage. Integration into the life of a team or a whole business is crucial for someone to settle in and go home feeling as though they have contributed something of value in their first days of being with you.

10. **Hunt for new skills.** You recruited them for a particular sales role and measured them against your job profile, but it's amazing how many other talents and skills are overlooked. In a smaller business these 'peripheral' skills can be truly transformative, if encouraged to show up alongside the ones you originally went fishing for. Interrogate them in the first week about their previous roles: what they learned and why that might be useful to you. You'll learn so much more than the job interview when their job offer was on the line. Give them a couple of months in the job, then ask them what skills they have that they're not using in the job. There's usually an unearthed gem that you can use elsewhere in the business.

This chapter is really about creating and sustaining excitement and value. Yes, there is genuine excitement about a new joiner – not just for you, but for them too. The commitment you put into their induction and the quality of planning they experience will keep this going for a long, long time.

Few things in business beat the feeling that you've recruited someone really good – someone you know positively impacts your business from month one and who the team are beginning to look up to.

25
What's A Sales Culture And Can I Have One?

If you're a gardener or know someone that is, you'll know it demands both patience and passion. The passion might be about creating a habitat for wildlife or sustaining a greenhouse full of germinating seeds, a compulsive search for that elusive clematis, or just about keeping the slugs off your lettuces. Whatever it is, it keeps gardeners poring over catalogues and kneeling in the mud long after their neighbours have abandoned their patios in favour of the warmth of their homes.

It's never about a quick fix, it's always about doing the right thing by nature and that's often about the right plant for the right place and not trying to force something to grow in a setting it hates. Seeds, cuttings and fully grown plants all thrive with this approach and will mutiny elsewhere.

Gardening and creating sales cultures have a lot in common. A commitment to tailoring the environment for its inhabitants to thrive. Ensuring the right inhabitants are in the right place and doing the right things. Having patience to learn and plan. Creating a team that blends and grows to produce something wonderful and the courage to change the scheme when something's not quite right with the overall effect. And all the time, remembering to nourish the environment, dig out the weeds and to prune as required to ensure everyone grows to their best potential without any one member overpowering the entire scheme.

So, if you're growing a sales culture and you can't find it in your local garden centre, where do you begin? Sales culture is the character and personality of a business beyond the boundaries of the people who have the word sales in their job titles. Few things make us more frustrated than hearing that customers are the job of the sales team.

A buzzing sales culture is the combination of:

- **Common purpose and goals:** Subscribing to a reason for being, a shared view of where the entire business is headed and why. Understanding that everyone, regardless of job title and department, has an important and distinct role to play in the success of sales, customer service and client retention.

- **Shared behaviours:** Sharing a set of beliefs relating to the terms and conditions for how teams operate together, and what constitutes a breach of these versus a fulfilment of these.

- **Ways of working:** Agreed procedures and processes that enable everyone to be certain of what they are doing and why. To have surety that others within their own team are also working in the same way, and that others beyond their team are working to support the end goal and customers.

- **Commitment and co-operation:** A willingness to put aside personal egos and departmental agendas for the sake of the business. Ensuring the whole team succeeds and that the skills and behaviours of every individual contribute to team success.

- **Resolution of disagreements:** Talking openly and frankly with a focus on the problem rather than the person to ensure issues are resolved effectively. Allowing people to express concerns and accepting that feedback is for the good of the team.

Boss watching

How trust shows up between the members of your team and across your business is crucial. If your people don't trust each other, then anything else you do will be wasted. When push comes to shove, there is no such thing as a surplus of trust, but there's certainly a price to be paid for too little.

Trust acts as an invisible accelerant right across a business. High levels of trust can help a slightly vague strategy or wobbly operational plan find its wings and fly, as the team will work harder and commit longer to ensuring results. Conversely, a fabulous strategy coupled with a beautifully gilded operational plan is still more likely to limp along or fail when trust has disintegrated. The fire and energy needed for implementation will be dowsed by disharmony, watchfulness and contradiction.

How the boss behaves is critical to trust. Boss watching is a sport that's universally enjoyed by staff. You set the tone for what's acceptable and what's not. You consciously or unconsciously role model behaviours and attitudes daily. There is no such thing as an off-camera moment when you own the place. The upside with boss watching is when you do great things, others do too.

If your team is watching you break your own commitments, let yourself off the hook, disrespect customers or generally wiggle out of things (or ask others to help you do this), how will they respond when trust gets mentioned? It can be helpful to share your own working foibles and quirks to help your team understand that these are not silent messages you are hoping they'll 'catch' via boss watching but your own little peculiarities that help you stay sane.

EARLY TO RISE

Lynne is pathologically early for everything in her world. 'On time' means late and creates needless stress for her, so every external client meeting will find Lynne practising her loitering skills nearby in a café or car park at least thirty minutes before the meeting is due to begin.

Explaining this to her team, with her expectation that 'on time' for them is ensuring they are seated, settled and ready to begin at the designated time, makes life easier. 'On time' is the standard. It prevents an entire team amending their definition of 'on time' to 'being 30 minutes early for everything because the boss is'.

Communicating what you expect of others is key. It's fine for the boss to clear emails late on a Sunday if that suits their lifestyle, but if they're telling others that a good work–life balance and looking after mental health are important, then their staff need to be told that the same isn't expected of them.

Building team trust

One simple way of accelerating a sales culture is for a team to agree expectations with each other. It's a straightforward, two-way conversation that will help reduce the need for guessing and mind reading within your teams and between you and them.

How you position this will depend upon the numbers in each of your teams, how much trust already exists, and whether there have been recent misunderstandings that this can help address directly. It may be more a general check-in and conversation to ensure that you understand each other. Ideally, you want this face to face and you need to let people know clearly and simply how you expect your teams to contribute on the day. You might say team members are expected to:

1. Be contributors

2. Communicate honestly

3. Co-operate with one another

4. Problem-solve together

5. Learn from one another

The conversation should cover day-to-day operations such as timekeeping, reporting, working together, and how they operate or respond when you're in meetings or just not immediately available. Make sure you share your expectations of how customers are served or responded to. This might be exactly the same list for each team within your business, but what's likely to differ is the specifics of how that shows up within each team and how they co-operate across your business.

Once a team is used to these conversations your challenge will be to stop them talking, but to begin with the following questions might help to kick-start the discussion. Having them think about answers in advance might make them more comfortable to share on the day itself.

Ten questions to explore sales culture:

1. How can the 'likes' of each member be brought out in our group?

2. How can we avoid the dislikes emerging? What will we do if they emerge?

3. How can each person's strengths be brought out?

4. How can we avoid individual weaknesses coming into play?

5. What do we need to do more of to ensure we continue to be happy and successful?

6. What do we need to do less of?

7. What do we expect (insert your name here) to do more of to help us?

8. What do we expect (insert your name here) to do less of to help us?

9. What do we expect more generally of our relationship with (insert your name here) and how we are managed?

10. What level of support do we expect handling tricky customers?

To get the best from this conversation let your team speak first. It ensures that you hear what they really mean and need rather than them trying to position their ideas to align with you if you share your expectations first. Ensure you explore answers to really understand the meaning behind the words. Nominating one of the team to capture comments on a flipchart ensures common understanding of what's said and encourages team ownership.

Start by agreeing those expectations that align between yours and the team's, or that you are happy with from the team. Where there is obvious and easy compromise, explore these next. Ensure you and the team compromise over these and that compromising is done by both sides. Where you cannot meet their expectations, be honest and say so directly. Explain why. Avoid vague half-excuses as this will dent the trust you're working on creating. If there is an alternative, offer it. If not, do not make one up.

After the meeting, document and share this agreement. Publish it for the team and use it as a touchstone for how you all behave, keep promises and work together. Ensure you and the team hold everyone accountable for its upkeep.

Sales culture: Greater than the sum of its parts

Really, sales culture is an intangible thing, though you know for sure when you've got it or when it's missing. The steps above help pull it together, but it's a theme that runs through all aspects of your business:

- How does our mission and purpose unite teams? (Chapter 17)

- Is our sales process built around the customer? (Chapter 30)

- How do we target and reward sales teams? (Chapter 28)

- Are we recruiting for cultural fit? (Chapter 23)

And so on – you get the picture.

26
How Do I Build A High-performing Sales Team?

Nothing beats the buzz of being part of a high-performing team. Whether that's the England cricket team winning the 2019 World Cup by the skin of their teeth and the bowling prowess of the newest and youngest member; mountain rescue volunteers putting their own safety at risk for a stranger as they dash up a fell in aid of an injured hiker, or dragon-boat racers eating up the miles and the competition on the water.

Energy radiates from them. The very act of coming together and being a team transcends every individual contribution. On first inspection it might resemble magic: the feeling that everyone knows where they fit within the team and that they trust everyone else to know that too. The common, almost unspoken understanding of where the team is headed, what it's doing and why. Frank conversations that drive high achievement, learning and success. It's not magic, of course, but deliberate intervention, with magical results.

There are great teams, good teams, mediocre teams and totally dysfunctional teams (when even the term 'team' becomes an oxymoron). High-performing teams are always greater than the sum of the parts. Truly dysfunctional ones can be so toxic and broken that they become lesser than the sum, with energy and effort directed to destruction, confusion and needless competition.

If you are truly committed to developing or retaining your high-performing sales team, some sustained effort is required. They are not a product of osmosis or accidentally discovering a shared love of Magnum ice-creams (although few teams will refuse them when offered). Teams behave like powerballs – the brightly coloured, dense rubbery type you had as a youngster that could pound off the pavement and head skywards above your neighbour's home. The greater the energy invested in how hard you threw that ball at the tarmac, the higher the chance you'd get it right over the roof and avoid the wrath of a parent having to go and rescue another lost ball. Teams are the same (except for the bit about bouncing them off pavements). To fly high they need energy and effort up front.

Evolution or revolution

The dynamics of a team evolve constantly. As their context or construct changes, how they work together, how they respond to each other and how they deliver results will also change. Every time there's a change in membership – a promotion, a new starter, a leaver – your sales team will reset. Regardless of how well it's performing before that change, introducing a new person to the team affects several elements that are vital for high performance. This is demonstrated clearly in team sports: big-money signings do not always improve the team.

How well the new member of the team understands their own position within the team, their fit within your business, and how quickly they establish social bonds with the other members of your team are key. These also affect how quickly the team recovers their equilibrium.

Ownership and aligned goals

What's often overlooked in team performance is the granting of authority to act. It sounds so simple, but many a team or an individual have energetically taken ownership of a sales goal only to find themselves reprimanded for overstepping the mark when they then get on with the achieving part of it.

Ensure everyone knows the scope of their authority alongside their goals so that they can concentrate on achieving them rather than chasing you for permission to try. It's also worth considering the wider measures and messages within your business: are they aligned to support your sales goals and activity, or do they contradict the behaviours and attitudes you're hoping to see?

If you really want your sales team to be flexible, creative risk-takers, how you respond to failure, left-field ideas and a lack of adherence to process or procedure is crucial. If you expect them to think, plan and work for the longer-term benefit of your business and clients, be mindful of how many short-term focus instructions or initiatives you lay across them. Resist examining everything through the lens of history, as this orientates people in the wrong direction. Link learning, goals and actions to the vision and purpose you have and ensure the team feel part of this by involving them in the shaping and creation of them.

The right tools

Arm your team with everything they need to succeed. Ensure they are supported by their technology and tools, rather than inhibited. If they are working with client design files, ensure they can view them and open them with the correct software. Saving the cost of software licenses and expecting them to load a file into a free web application that takes three clicks, two attempts and five minutes of humming, while watching a blank screen load, is like asking a top rider to master dressage on a donkey. Nothing fits properly, the harness is too big, the stirrups too long and you can't plait its tousled mane. No Olympic Gold is ever going to be forthcoming, and both rider and donkey will soon stop trying.

The same goes for hardware, software, sales tools and telephony systems. Anything crucial to the job should be the most up to date that you can afford. If you can automate repeating administrative tasks, so much the better. Every industry is different, but increasingly the ability to capture, store and derive insight from customer data is becoming a factor in an organisation's ability to compete. You might not yet need a full subscription to Salesforce or LinkedIn Sales Navigator, but make sure you know what they do and how they could help you.

At the same time also ensure that your team has easy access to all of the information they need to succeed. If they are held accountable and rewarded for the profit they generate, ensure it's readily available to them (traffic lighted or within dashboards to make it easy to understand).

The right skills

How and where you invest in developing your people will be unique to you. Making the wrong choice offers a plethora of bespoke ways of wasting your time and money on the wrong learning, the wrong person or the wrong skills. Making the right choice can be transformative for all involved.

What's crucial is that your sales team have all the skills they need to achieve the goals they are pursuing. If they are charged with achieving profitable sales how will they achieve this if they don't at least understand the basics of profit and loss and have some idea of how cost works?

On first inspection it might be tempting to train a team or a sales person who struggles with converting new enquiries into booked orders with a series of funky closing techniques. But if, on closer inspection, you discover that the root cause is related to their ability to listen and ask curious questions, then training a new set of closing techniques will change nothing other than your bank balance.

There is often a marked difference between the symptoms observed and the root cause. Taking time to investigate, test and consider what sits behind the result or behaviour you see will help you identify the support required. Sometimes the root cause isn't a lack of skill at all. If your investigation identifies that it's the quality of the leads your team are being handed by your AdWords campaign, then spending time addressing this could offer far greater returns than spending money on training how to close a sale.

A root cause can be many things – a broken process, a lack of knowledge, misaligned or poor-quality input or a lack of a key sales tool. Some may require training, but others might just need you to change what's going on in your business so that success can happen more easily.

The importance of feedback and coaching

There are plenty of teams out there who can describe in a hundred different ways how they are blamed and have their failures pointed out in regular, painful detail. They will also tell you that praise and thank you rarely show up. Others will describe their worlds as being within a 'tsunami of telling' where tasks and instructions pour down upon them.

This doesn't mean becoming the purveyor of hugs at every turn. Praise should always mean something and have some worth. If a team suspects you of random praise giving, then what you offer will quickly become a worthless currency. Frankness, transparency and honesty in praise, in feedback and in the admission of failure is key. Use every opportunity to check in with your sales team (and your wider business) for feed-back, thoughts and musings. Good and bad.

Coaching underpins the development and continued growth of your people and your business. Listening to calls and offering insight. Observing presentations and offering suggestions for improvement. Joining a meeting and identifying underplayed strengths that could be leveraged to greater effect. All these contribute to creating a powerful sales culture. Asking questions that provoke thinking, reflection and ownership help engender a culture of improvement and accountability – something telling never will.

Businesses with this culture buzz. There's conta-gious energy. Your people respond with care to your customers and will fight their corner to ensure the right things get done for them and by them. Your teams know exactly what they are doing and are getting on with being successful.

Motivating sales meetings

Regular, planned, sales meetings are a must. By regular we mean weekly or fortnightly, not the yearly pilgrimages to the dental hygienist that for most of us are made under duress.

Whether your sales team is office- or home-based, bringing everyone together and lifting them out of their daily focus is important. Home-based teams, in particular, require effort to establish them into a supportive, cohesive unit. Working on your own every day can become a lonely and isolating place to be without the support of other voices on the end of a phone, a face on Zoom or the opportunity to meet up.

Sales meetings should allow everyone a voice, enabling your team to shape and share strategy or to plan and review the execution of that strategy. Meetings are an opportunity to review progress, to unpick learning and to connect with each other and grow. Most of all, meetings should be designed to enhance the team, to energise your people and to create momentum and motivation. Regardless of the actual content of the meeting, the needs of your people and your team should be of utmost importance. Keep meetings visual, collaborative, honest and engaging.

Build these conversations around customers. Nothing inspires the team more than being able to bring back insight from the people that really matter to them. It's also a great opportunity for you to hear first-hand what's really happening in the real world.

Shaping agendas around decisions, problem-solving and outcomes helps focus a team on success and provides milestones to track their progress. Ensure ideas that emerge from these discussions are implemented so that you create continuous improvement.

Avoid excuses. Account for results with reasons, learn from them and move on.

Including other departments in these meetings creates understanding and wider collaboration and if you want the entirety of your business to see sales as being part of their roles too, this is a great way to support and encourage this perspective.

Imagine being a sales team targeted and rewarded on the gross profit of each of your sales to customers. You work hard to understand their needs, create a quote that differentiates you from your competition in what is a crowded market, and celebrate when they place their order with you. Imagine knowing that if that order is produced in-house (the way you specified it with your client and agreed with your production manager) the profit you earn will enhance your salary by a reasonable number of pounds. Now imagine how it would feel to have production mis-schedule your order, fail to meet the delivery date, and then declare that it needs to be sent to a third party to be produced. Goodbye gross profit.

In the rules of how your commission works – you take the hit. Production feels little or no pain for this decision and you earn zero commission. That's why your entire business needs to believe sales is part of their jobs too.

These are some basic questions that you can use to structure your sales agenda:

- How are we doing against our goals and measures?

- How does this impact our plan?

- What's happened with our key customers (good and bad)?

- What have we learned this week?

- What problems do we need to solve today?

- Who's doing what next week?

- How does this impact other departments?

- How are we doing as a team?

Launching the powerball

Remember to always be on the search for talent. If you bump into someone with the right attitude and skills for your business, ask whether you can create a space. Parallel with that, constantly ask your team what more they can give. What skills are they keeping hidden? The cheapest way of attracting talent is by growing the people you already have. Secondly, set the dial accurately on the balance between results and team: Most sales people are competitive, and you want to harness that, but the process needs to be calibrated so individuals can give their best without playing against the rest of the team.

Finally, don't be afraid of being tough. If you've given people the right goals, tools and coaching you have the right to call them out when performance falls short. It might seem contradictory, but being friends with everyone doesn't actually work in building high performance. It's been shown over and again that what wins leaders the respect of their teams is dealing with poor performance quickly and effectively.

Follow these principles and the powerball is ready for lift-off.

27
What's My Customer Journey?

One person's 'tomayto' is another's 'tomahto', as Fred Astaire sang in the famous ditty.

The customer journey is so full of buzzwords right now that it's difficult to differentiate between them. Are you selling in a multichannel world or are you going omnichannel? Do you need to focus on customer experience (CX to those in the know) or user experience (UX), and is that the same as customer journey?

There has been such an extraordinary shift in the online experience in just a few short years that much of this terminology is driven by the digital world. Customers are moving to online platforms in droves and there is a veritable army of digital specialists looking to service their needs. Your inbox and LinkedIn feed will not be short of offers from prospective agencies offering services from website design to social media planning to CX mapping. Honestly, it's exhausting.

Customers versus consumers

First things first. Are you selling to consumers (ie the public) or are you selling to another business (usually described as B2B)? This will influence all sorts of decisions in your business from where you find customers through to how you conduct transactions with them and onto how legislation applies to your sales. Terminology is important.

In the UK most retailers refer to people visiting their stores as customers. If you're a craft brewer making cans of beer, then the retailer is your customer and the people visiting stores probably referred to as shoppers. The consumer is the one who drinks the beer. Lucky them.

To optimise your sales, you want to understand three customer journeys:

1. The professional buyers employed by Tesco, Wetherspoons, Planet Organic, etc – buy the beer.

2. The shopper – pays for the beer.

3. The consumer – drinks the beer.

Depending on your business, one will probably be more important than the others. Start there. What you're probably seeing already is that the expectations of buyers (the professionals) are being shaped by their experience as consumers. A typical illustration of this is a buyer in the construction industry we spoke with. Our brief was to help him improve service to building sites across the nation. His benchmark wasn't muddy fields though, it was beds.

The week before he'd been online, paid for a new bed with his credit card and booked a delivery slot. The bed arrived, was delivered to the room he specified, unpacked and all rubbish removed. 'That,' he said, 'is service.' We all had our heads in our hands as he described the contrasting building site experience of vans delivering to the wrong plot, product being 'shorted' and missing paperwork.

When did you last sit up and notice 'wow' service? Was it in your industry or elsewhere? It's worth continually asking yourself what best practice really is in your sector. It's as likely shaped by your customer's experience of Amazon, Uber or Monzo as it is by what your big, well-funded competitor does. Think big.

Multichannel versus omnichannel

Specialists in the subject will try to tell you that there is a distinction between these definitions, but you can use whichever word you choose. The important question is whether or not you do it well.

Retail is the sector that is perhaps most frequently spoken about as being multichannel. At its simplest level it's clear that a Halfords – with stores on retail parks and a swish website – is operating in at least two channels. Banking is finding this hard to adjust to, with a legacy of high street outlets that politicians are keen to see remain. Meanwhile, people are using less cash, reducing demand for cashpoints (another channel) and conducting transactions online. Most businesses with costly legacy systems are finding it tough to adjust in the face of new market entrants who can excel in one channel.

There are questions to answer about the corporate responsibility, employee care and environmental impact of many of the so-called global disrupter businesses, but there is no denying the esteem in which they are held by customers for the way they have transformed the customer experience. Uber doesn't own taxis but has a fabulous app.[29] Amazon doesn't own vans but is obsessive about the customer service of their drivers.[30] Monzo doesn't own a single bank

29 M Iqbal, 'Uber revenue and usage statistics' (Business of Apps, 30 October 2020), www.businessofapps.com/data/uber-statistics, accessed 16 January 2021
30 The DO School, '"Customer obsession" is key to Amazon's success' (Medium, 9 May 2019), https://medium.com/purposeful-retail/customer-obsession-is-key-to-amazons-success-4d01e062fd72, accessed 16 January 2021

but has engaged customers like no high street bank.[31] All these examples demonstrate the importance of winning in the channel you need to succeed in. If your channels don't join up then you either incur management costs double-handling sales, or worse, you disappoint customers.

So what?

Despite all this new-fangled terminology, the questions you need to answer remain relatively straightforward. Yes, you can spend a fortune piecing together data from myriad digital touchpoints, but even then, the insight you're trying to gain is how you excite customers.

In our consulting work we focus on what we call the Customer Flywheel. What are the measures that clearly demonstrate your customer is choosing you ahead of your competitors? In a B2B market your products and services should be wrapped in a message that clearly identifies how you make your customers' lives easier. You want to excite them? Either you help them deliver growth, or you support them to do something notably faster or cheaper.

31 'Finder Banking Customer Satisfaction Awards 2019' (Finder, 2019), www.finder.com/uk/bank-accounts/finder-banking-customer-awards-2019, accessed 16 January 2021

The insight you have to achieve this will vary widely by industry:

Fast-moving consumer goods (FMCG): You can access shopper behavioural data that shows how people buying your product are worth more to a retailer than your competitors. Maybe they are high-spending families or perhaps they show greater loyalty to your brand and will shop around if not satisfied.

Nothing interests a retailer more than a robust demonstration of how your product helps attract more people to their stores, spending more and visiting more often.

Construction: There is much less published data than in FMCG, but the end job is more transparent. It's not easy to establish how and when families use your cornflakes, but you can chat with a plumber about how much it costs to fit out a bathroom and how long it takes.

Armed with this sort of insight, you can build a story about whole-job costs that shows how your innovative all-in-one bath and toilet saves money. Yes, the system might come with a higher price tag, but installing it in half the time saves money overall. Ask most people in the UK what skirting board is made from and they'll tell you it's wood. No longer. It's now mainly made of MDF – not because MDF is notably different in price from wood, but because its smooth surface makes it quicker to sand and paint. The whole-job costs are significantly lower.

These examples are from widely different industries but the strategic principle is the same. Think less about your product or service and interrogate deeply how the end user (parent or plumber) can be encouraged to use more. What's the value for them?

Delivering the customer journey

CX demands a truly single-minded obsession about the customer. How happy do you feel about your customer experience? Customers, whether B2B or business to consumer (B2C) don't care about your job titles, departmental boundaries or team away days. They are motivated only by what comes out of your organisation. Is it delivered to a high quality (ethically as well as physically), on time and at a competitive price?

It follows from here that the companies most successfully delivering the customer journey don't view customers as 'something that sales do'. Sure, the sales team will be leading day-to-day communication, but the whole organisation will be lined up behind them. Goals and reward can be synchronised with this. Why not bonus everyone in your organisation on customer satisfaction measures or build it into how you rate their performance? It could represent just a small percentage of any bonus, but it sure will focus minds.

It might sound a little brutal, but if people in HR, IT and finance aren't in some way accountable for the sales numbers, then aren't they just running an expensive governance process? What could you do to have people outside sales more involved with customer management?

In our experience, most people in non-sales jobs relish the opportunity to be involved in customer projects. It excites them to be involved in something they view as important and provides a valuable and balanced perspective to the sales team. In fact, some of the best sales directors we've met didn't start out in sales – individuals with backgrounds as diverse as HR, engineering and the British army. None of them were selling experts, but all of them were smart enough to listen to what customers needed and to build an organisation obsessive about delivering it.

YOU CAN'T RUSH THE BOARD

As part of some sales process work, we helped a small tech company, Systech, to think about customer journey. Easy first step? We held a workshop and invited some of their key customers.

The big insight coming out of this session was friction around finalising the order. Systech were frustrated that, having specified a job and submitted a detailed quote they were then kept waiting weeks for the decision to go ahead. The client, on the other hand, didn't appreciate being chased for confirmation when they were trying to navigate internal approval and sign-off procedures. You can't rush the board.

Between them they figured out a means of structuring the quote in a way that made it easier to approve. Then they actively sought out relationships with the decision-makers before key dates.

Without going all Pharrell Williams, a great customer journey makes everyone happy. Customers are happy to be listened to; internal teams are happy to contribute to great customer experience and the sales team are happy with the positive buzz this creates.

When did you last ask your customers how happy they are with your service?

28
What Are The Best Sales KPIs?

Most business owners will be aware of the idea that strategy is about deciding what not to do. It doesn't translate that way in reality, of course, because we're all too busy keeping customers happy, covering staff absence and cracking jokes with the accountant. But few of us would deny that focusing on a few important things and doing them well is the route to success. It's not the principle we disagree with, just a wavering of discipline when it comes to making it happen.

Less is more

So it is with sales. Sitting in a management meeting with that comical accountant and surrounded by spreadsheets, we know there are a whole range of metrics that we need to juggle to keep the business on track. Revenue, profit... Is that net or gross? How far my sales person is driving and how many calls they make. How effectively my sales people convert leads into suspects into prospects. And there's no mercy if they don't capture that in the CRM system...

Most sales people value consistent goals and simple measures. Less is more. Give them a straightforward target, the tools to do the job and encourage them on their way. The problem comes when you begin to notice the first signs of a sales tangle. Growth isn't quite where you want it to be and you get the sense that commitment isn't quite what it was a few months before. Your new sales manager was a breath of fresh air when she joined the business, but now she's coming up to a year and your hunch is you're starting to get excuses. You want to get 'closer to the sales numbers' – but which sales numbers?

If this isn't something you've spent much time on previously (and there's often good reason why you don't), then start with a two-tier system. Apply the less is more principle to the measures you openly assess your team against. Meanwhile, study in more depth the activity metrics that might be affecting the headline numbers. Take the time to check these suppositions before you baffle the team with what might prove to be initial hunches. You don't really want to be debating this with them.

It may sound obvious, but the first thing with KPIs is to ensure you will be happy if they are achieved. Our client, Design Ltd, relied on frequent project wins to deliver their sales number, so commissions were high, yet the MD frequently complained about the soft sales targets which meant he was stressing about hitting budget while his sales team pocketed big bonus payments. The numbers didn't add up. Achieving KPI targets *must* mean the company hits its business plan.

High-level sales KPIs

These are the three headline sales measures to consider at a total business level:

1. **Gross profit or sales:** Sales revenue isn't the worst target to set a sales team, though if you can easily generate some sort of profit number that will be more useful. Even a simple gross profit that takes cost of goods from selling price will help to focus them on what you can bank rather than what they can sell.

2. **Customer satisfaction:** Easier to measure in consumer businesses than some B2B industries, but critical to your future success. Look at online reviews (TripAdvisor, Amazon, Reviews.co.uk, etc) or gather direct feedback from key accounts about how they rate you.

3. **One key activity measure:** Select something that means you're measuring the team both on their effectiveness as well as their output (sales or profit), for example, number of quotes issued or conversion rate.

Detailed sales metrics

Once you've mastered the headline measures then you can and should keep track of a whole basket of sales metrics like net margin, average order size and acquisition cost behind the scenes.

In some industries it will be important to measure the number of days within which your invoices are settled to ensure cashflow is working for the business; in others, things like customer retention rates and lifetime value might be key, but keep it simple for the team. It's up to you whether you report this visually or in some sort of spreadsheet. We've seen both work and it depends only on your personal preference.

Below is an example of our Sales Benchmark report, which is the spreddie format of sales KPI monitoring. You may not assess all these measures or you may want more. The choice is yours.

Benchmark	Data Availability	Source	Performance
Customer			
TripAdvisor star rating	Good	TripAdvisor	On target
Company-level data			
Sales performance	Good	Management info	On target
Gross profit	Good	Management info	Below target
No. of orders	Good	Management info	Above target
Average order size	Good		
New/existing split	Etc	Etc	Etc
Selling cost			
Individual-level data			
Sales vs target			
Gross profit			

Alternatively, you can capture all these numbers in a series of graphs – whatever works best for you and your team.

Input/output goals

These detailed sales metrics can either be input- or output-based but whichever you use will have a marked impact upon how your sales team act. An input goal focuses upon the activity: call a minimum of fifteen new prospects per day. An output goal focuses upon the results achieved: achieve new client sales of £4,500 per month.

Input goals carry risk in that they can often be achieved despite the result. Hurrah, fifteen calls a day were made. Alas, they were poor quality leads, few of whom were your target customer profile. Worse, your team rarely spoke with the decision-maker. But hurrah – they all successfully made fifteen calls a day and you hit your target...

If you want to use input goals, be sure to understand the dynamics of the processes behind the scenes. If you work back that £4,500 target to input goals, you will need to understand things like:

- How many calls are being made?

- How often do calls reach decision-makers?

- How many proposals are being made?

- How many quotes are accepted?

- What is the average first order size?

Having this information may then tell you that you need a different activity target for the number of calls being made or you need better quality leads. Maybe you need better sales tools, or your team need training in a key sales step. From this, you can shape input goals, but they require constant vigilance to ensure the assumptions you have used to create them remain valid and the results remain as expected.

Output goals bring different challenges. They ascribe ownership to the sales person and team for the activity and hold them accountable for the results (the output). This assumes that your sales team understand the exact meaning of the goal. You'd be surprised how many ways 'Increase qualified opportunities by 20%' can be misunderstood.

When you've tracked the scorecard long enough to know certain measures work well, then it's time to share with the team. This can be a helpful step in identifying pockets of talent in the team and showcasing these skills within the business. They're also great for one-to-one meetings with the team where you're trying to improve performance.

Keep it simple

Have you ever been tempted to add multiple levels of measures? You're the boss and can measure all sorts of things, so you start dabbling. Over time you add different layers and eventually you're not sure what is driving the business and what's the smoke screen. If in any doubt, focus just on the three headline measures. Directors frequently ask us to help with this and the relief is remarkable. The detailed sales metrics are fascinating and can help identify specific improvements, but after what can be years of tracking every metric, measuring each team member and logging every action you can ease the strain by simply focusing on the big picture.

Keep it simple, up to date, and error free: sales, profit, primary activity. In summary, if you're in any doubt about KPIs, then err on the side of simplicity. You can always add more later.

29

How Do I Get The Best Price For My Products And Services?

This is one of the classic sales questions. Price is possibly the biggest single determinant of what the future shape of your business will be. The reason? Virtually everything you do in business costs, but add a penny (or better, a pound) to the price of your product and the whole penny drops straight to your bottom line. No additional costs, no extra resource, just profit.

Do you believe customers are paying what your product or service is really worth? In assessing pricing policy there are three component parts to think about and approaching these in harmony will give you the best way of maximising price and profit:

- Net price

- Gross profit

- Cost of selling

Net price

What's your net price? In many cases list price or recommended price will be virtually irrelevant. What matters is your actual realised price: what you make from selling your product after you've concluded discussing all those pesky discounts that customers asked for. If you start with list price, then you need to take off all discounts to evaluate the net price. That's discount off list (applied to every invoice for big customers), promotion funds, settlement discounts, overriders and rebates. It's often a sizeable list, so let's look at these in more detail.

Net price watch-outs

In the consumer goods industry, promoting is a full-time job, with millions of pounds spent reducing the price of your cereals, drinks and toilet rolls in Tesco et al. In many other industries it's common practice to discount or promote products at given times and it's worth considering how this activity impacts on net price. Not every one of these factors will apply in all industries, but because the consumer goods industry

(FMCG) is so advanced in this area it's worth looking at them as a benchmark.

Ensure consistent measures: Plenty of buyers and numerous vendors of sales service will be quick to tell you that a spend of X returns a sales uplift of Y. In evaluating promotion spend, you must remember to measure the incremental profitability of the transaction, not just the sales uplift.

The cost of doing business: Many powerful customers make you believe that promotions are an implicit part of the deal. Fashions vary, but there have been periods when Tesco, Boots and others expected deals like 'Buy One Get One Free' as a designated part of the listing package. Ocado, which doesn't have the shelf space constraints of some retailers, can be a relatively easy place to achieve a listing, but they expect a contribution towards marketing funding as part of the deal. You are in effect paying them to reach your own customers. It's a nasty shock to the founders of many small, entrepreneurial businesses. Is there an alternative? In many cases, no. Assessing the ROI of precisely what activity you undertake and testing out alternatives is one way of minimising the downside. Beyond that, you need to place it in the context of your overall prize with that customer – the lifetime value – and decide whether or not you want to afford it.

Impact on your other products: It's staggering how many FMCG businesses don't understand this. On literally any visit to a major supermarket you'll be able to find a brand offering a promotion on one product which is guaranteed to steal from another part of the range. For years we never paid full price for Ambrosia custard because when the cartons were full price, the tins were discounted and vice versa. It was as good as guaranteed. The most painful examples of this for suppliers are where you realise it's cheaper to buy two small packs rather than one large one. Not only is the consumer walking away with the discount, but the supplier is incurring two lots of packaging cost, making the deal doubly expensive.

What happens after the promotion? The key consideration here is what impact your short-term discount has on end user behaviour. It doesn't matter whether you're selling biscuits or bandages: if the consumer doesn't use any more then you haven't sold any more. Not by the end of the year when monthly sales are averaged out. All product categories behave differently and it's important to understand your own dynamics, but the oft-quoted example is never to reduce the price of a toilet roll. You can sell as cheaply as you wish, but nobody uses any extra because it was a great deal.

Competitor behaviour: In some markets this isn't visible, but it's worth keeping a tracking document where you can lay hands on it. In part it relates to the previous point: often your competitor promotes in the month before or after the one in which you do.

Sometimes that's deliberate, but it may simply be a function of the customer not wanting to promote all brands simultaneously. If you average your net price over a year then you want to understand both the impact of the discount you give when you're promoting and the reduced volume you sell at full price when your competitor discounts.

Gross profit

The second element is the cost of providing the goods or service – what many businesses call gross profit. It's usually calculated as sales revenue minus cost of goods; likely to include material costs, production and labour costs, though probably not capital items like the cost of buying production equipment. It's quite common to see companies with a gross profit of over 50%, which over the years has prompted many owners to splash out prematurely on a new company car.

Cost of selling

The third consideration – and in our experience the one least likely to be measured – is the cost of selling. At a total business level, the accountant will be looking at this as it's wrapped up in overhead cost but they might not be scrutinising it at a customer level, which is where it's most valuable.

Total selling cost is made up of obvious items like sales salaries and bonuses, but you might also decide it includes marketing and part of your HR and finance costs. Each case is different, but if you sum them all up to work out the average cost per order it can give really interesting insight. Dig a level deeper and you start to understand how expensive each customer really is. How much does it cost you to resolve price queries with that customer who always deducts from invoice? How much is it costing you when one of your sales people spends five minutes longer on a call than another?

Pulling together these three areas optimises price for your business. There's obviously a reasonably heavy analytical aspect to this, so someone who can make sense of numbers is valuable but the key is in the making sense. This can be a hugely complicated exercise, but once again the 'What does this mean?' is about making something happen.

Whether it's encouraging your buying team to think differently about purchase price or whether it's encouraging sales not to give away discounts so easily, it needs someone who understands the commercial relationships, not just the spreddie.

You might know of industries where a price increase is as simple as telling customers they'll be paying more from next month. Most are not as simple as this and there's a pretty complicated dance ritual between customer and supplier before agreement is reached.

If asked to work in detail on a price increase for a client we focus on what we call the eight vital workstreams in delivering a price increase:

- Negotiation scenarios
- Cost rationale
- Pack strategy and production flex
- Competitor and price elasticity
- Promotion calendar and compliance
- Customer profit modelling
- Channel strategy and scheduling
- Legal compliance

Just a quick glance at this list demonstrates that managing price optimally is a true team effort. It needs sales, marketing, legal, production: people with a mix of talents and skills to work through the vital plan components and make sure it is implemented on time and predictably.

Ten ways to land a price increase

1. **Lead from the top:** A successful price increase discussion is not just about the sales function and

it needs visible senior leadership to ensure cross-functional teams are pulling together.

2. **Crunch the detail:** There's a heap of planning in a successful price increase – price elasticity, impact on business plans, channel priority etc – that needs the right level of skilled resource before any conversations open up with customers.

3. **Keep a sense of perspective:** If your price increase meeting is booked for an afternoon slot, chances are the buyer has already had a similar conversation that day. It might be years since you asked for an increase, but for any seasoned buyer it's their day job, so don't stress out your team.

4. **Use statistics responsibly (aka the customer knows more than you):** In the internet age many businesses know how supplier costs have changed and when, which means this needs to be a transparent conversation. Claiming that 'input cost A is 23% more expensive than three years ago' usually elicits a five- or ten-year chart showing a different trend.

5. **Comply with the law:** Consumer businesses can and should set a recommended retail price (RRP) for their product but cannot prevent a retailer from charging more (or less). Most industries have competition or promotion rules that affect pricing. Don't get caught out.

6. **Partnerships are only as good as the deal:** You might have a preferred relationship with your

customer and at times of genuine industry pressure this might help smooth the path of a price increase, but partnership or not, if the deal doesn't work for them it doesn't work. See if your contacts can advise on the 'What ifs?' before tabling the final proposal.

7. **Never take a price increase off the table:** By all means renegotiate your trading terms package to ensure that both parties are happy with the new commercial agreement, but if you back out of a price increase discussion your business loses credibility for a generation. Not to mention the implied question mark against the key account manager's negotiating skills...

8. **Never let the sales director negotiate:** If price increase discussions get messy then it can be helpful to involve senior teams to ensure there is a dialogue with the customer about the long-term direction of the business, but if you allow negotiations to escalate there are bigger reputations to protect.

9. **What's in it for me:** The spreadsheet nature of the work involved means price increases tend to become internally focused. Ultimately the end user of your product will decide whether it's worth the price, but ensuring there is some benefit for the customer in passing on your price increase will speed its adoption.

10. **Be confident:** If you've followed steps one to nine, you're well-prepared and have a robust case and can approach major customers with a positive story. This is one of those guidelines where reverse logic also holds true: if you're not confident, you probably shouldn't be asking.

Pricing is tough to get right but its significance is so great it bears this extra analysis. Hand on heart, can you say you've never faced a pricing tangle? We've worked with many companies on this. Some of them global, household name businesses that you'd never think would be worried about price. Others are small, local operators who have a hunch their goods and services are worth more.

In every case being confident about prices charged brings a sense of calm to the leaders of the organisation. You're in control of one of the key metrics in your business. You've found customers who love what you do and you're slowly getting the feeling that they actually appreciate its value.

30

Can You Help Me Build An Efficient Sales Funnel... Or Do I Mean Sales Process?

Potayto. Potahto. It's another of those Fred Astaire moments.

There is so much terminology about sales funnel, sales process and sales pipeline that it can all become a bit technical. Ask experts in the field and they will be adamant that your sales funnel is not the same thing as your sales pipeline. Worse, they will insist you're about to make expensive business mistakes if you confuse the two.

If you're the sales director of a large organisation with disparate sales teams then you do need to be clear on the distinction between – and the inter-relationship of – your high-level sales measures and the activities of your teams on the ground.

For small businesses, though, we think this is a good time to return to the 'What does this mean?' Simply, whether you call it funnel, process or pipeline, you want sales metrics to answer three questions:

1. What activities are my sales team undertaking?

2. Are these activities effective?

3. Do these activities give me confidence that we'll hit next week's (or next month's/next year's) sales number?

Most organisations will capture this data in a CRM system (we do) – just don't be tempted to believe that an expensive upgrade will necessarily answer the questions posed. Find a simple way of answering these questions and focus on improving the outcome of each.

For the purpose of this chapter, then, we'll use the terms interchangeably. Just be aware that purists will be more specific in their definitions.

What activities are my sales team undertaking?

Broadly speaking we all know what activities a sales team do. Whether they are ringing or visiting customers or whether they are contacting prospects or existing customers, the steps are similar.

We know (or hope) that they are identifying customer needs, understanding their problems, making presentations, closing sales... The list is long. What's not always clear is the order in which these happen and whether they make it more likely you'll achieve a sale. How confident do conversations with your sales people leave you feeling? Do you know they'll deliver – or hope they will?

If you're selling IT support, for example, an enthusiastic sales person could be discussing potential new laptops with a client but without aligning this with your tech team you've suddenly wound up the client about tech that doesn't actually suit their software needs and isn't supported by their imminent upgrade.

One of the key objectives of structuring a sales funnel is to apply something quantitative to the sales team's activity. It's a natural temptation for sales people to have a friendly cuppa with a prospect and conclude a sale is more likely as a result. It's often not, and you can get through many months of Typhoo and Bahlsen without actually moving any closer to a sale.

A structured approach forces the team to use a checklist approach that avoids kidding themselves that the kettle is on and the order imminent. You can identify and order the steps you need your sales person to complete before an order is confirmed. They'll vary by company and market, but should include things like:

- Complete credit check.

- Identify scope of customer project.

- Confirm budget holder and/or decision-maker.

- Hold face to face meeting or phone conversation.

- Submit quote.

Over time you and your team will figure out the best order in which these need to happen and what difference they make. Which leads us to effectiveness.

Are these activities effective?

This is what's classically referred to as the sales funnel part of the discussion. Again, there are some variations in how businesses define this, but this is a fairly standard diagram of a sales funnel.

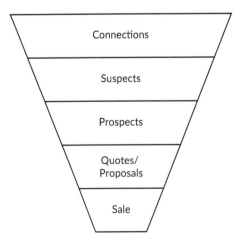

The efficiency of sales activities is measured by the shape of this funnel. Once you attach percentages to each stage of the funnel you can attach numbers to efficiency at each stage. The measurement works whether you're operating entirely in the digital world or whether you're selling in person, though the numbers will be different.

Let's say you regularly attend local networking meetings and generate leads through conversations with people you meet. You typically get to ten meetings each month and make around ten connections at each. Conveniently for this calculation, that's 100 business cards per month. 100 people are aware of you.

Your product is of wide interest to people, so you might find twenty people each month who you suspect might be worth following up with and you drop them a short email after meeting.

Of these, five come back to you expressing an interest and you can fix up a coffee and chat. Prospects. You know you're persuasive when in front of someone, so are confident that five meetings will enable you to issue three quotes.

Competition is tough in your market and some people just sell on price, so for every three quotes you reckon you'll receive one order. After all those meetings, bacon baps and coffees you have found one new client.

Good job. But a tough job.

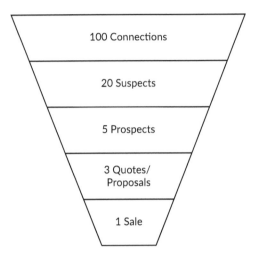

The effectiveness question, then, is about how you can improve the ratios at every stage of this funnel. What if you could better identify the one customer who eventually said 'yes' and focus your energy on finding more of them?

This is where many businesses will draw a comparison with the online customer journey. If you decided instead to generate leads via Google AdWords, the shape of this funnel could change entirely. You might not be too concerned about awareness, but AdWords could deliver 100 enquiries a month – that's five times your current level of suspects. You free up all that networking time and have an empty diary to close the deal on the glut of sales quotes you expect to issue.

The critical question is how good those leads are. Understanding whether networking leads convert better than AdWords leads and benchmarking that against the cost of each is what determines the effectiveness of your funnel.

The reverse sales funnel

It's worth pausing at this point to stress the impact of how a sales funnel works in reverse. Most businesses have ambitious sales targets, and the sales funnel metrics can identify how achievable these might be.

Let's say you want to grow the business by £100,000 this year. The one order you generated from all that networking last month is worth £2,000, so you'll need fifty new orders this year to hit your sales target.

Work backwards up the sales funnel and that means you'll need to:

- Issue 150 quotes.

- Attend 250 sales meetings with prospects (that's one a day).

- Email 1,000 suspects.

- Meet 5,000 people at fifty network events – phew!

What this helps you figure out is whether that sales growth is realistic and the resources you'll need to deliver it. Unless you have an expandable diary, it doesn't seem likely that you'll be able to attend all those network meetings and follow-up calls. Not while you're doing the day job. The cost of a sales person to generate and handle the extra leads therefore needs to be factored into the year's growth projections.

Am I confident I can hit my sales target?

The reverse sales funnel concept shows why we feel the need to ask this question.

What also comes into play here is the GIGO sales model, which as finance managers and CRM experts both know, stands for 'garbage in, garbage out'. It's a recurring complaint from people we work with that they don't have confidence in the sales funnel. It's not the funnel that's at fault, it's the flaky input that drives the reports that's to blame.

Business leaders are told by confident sales people that next month's number is stable. Then as next month becomes this month, they are just halfway to the target with three-quarters of the month gone. Uncomfortable.

It takes some robust analysis to ensure that the sales funnel (process or pipeline) is working efficiently and delivering accurate outputs, but it can be done. Below is a simple sales funnel that captures the steps outlined in the scenario above. A functioning business will need to add more detail to the right-hand column to reflect the working practices of their industry, but this is a start.

The percentages are taken directly from the calculations in the original funnel. It takes twenty suspects to deliver one order, so the conversion rate is 5%.

What this structure does is to provide more certainty by removing the 'cup of tea and biscuit' factor. When your sales person achieves all the steps in each criteria box, they can change the status of the customer from say, suspect to prospect – but not before. Hot drinks are not criteria.

Status	Likelihood	Criteria
SUSPECT	5%	EXPLORATORY
(Your email list after the network meeting)	(Typically, one in twenty becomes a sale)	• Client known to us (networking meeting) • Client works in our target industry and geography • Email sent
PROSPECT	20%	ESTABLISH CLIENT NEEDS
(The people you have coffee with)	(Typically, one in five becomes a sale)	• Client needs our type of product to operate effectively • Client meeting held • Decision-maker known and part of meeting
PROPOSAL	35%	PRICING AND PROPOSAL
(The people you send a quote to)	(Typically, one in three becomes a sale)	• Client specification agreed • Project timeline agreed • Formal quote issued
ORDER	100%	CONFIRMED AND DOCUMENTED ORDER
		• Purchase order no. is confirmed • Project start date confirmed in writing • Payment schedule agreed

How frequently do you feel the frustration of the unreliable sales funnel? An unpredictable sales number is one of the things most likely to damage the relationship between a sales person (or manager) and those running the business. Owners, accountants and factories all love predictability and it's a source of massive frustration when the number they were expecting isn't delivered. It's the emotional rollercoaster that peaks with every positive chat with the sales team, then plummets with each order that's delayed or buyer that's moved on. You're left with what feel like excuses.

It's a real boost for business owners to figure out some simple metrics around this. It sounds simple but we've had business owners beaming from ear to ear because we helped them structure the sales funnel in a way that reflects how their business really works. Gone are the days of second-guessing whether your sales person is naive, optimistic or a bad judge of character. In its place is something you might be able to take to the bank. Happy days.

Conclusion

The power of three is well known as a means of creating compelling messaging. From ancient religion to modern-day communication it's an accepted means of making language more persuasive. From, 'Faith, hope and charity' and, 'It's a mere hop, skip and a jump' to Julius Caesar's, 'I came, I saw, I conquered', it's used to emphasise a point with hidden rhythm. It's a rhythm that extends into the world of sales.

Sales solutions are the constant intertwining of three principles: Plan. People. Do. Bigger businesses might use different terminology like strategy, capability and execution, but it doesn't take away from the fact there are three vitally inter-related activities here.

Questions like, 'Who are my most important customers?' and, 'How do I get the best price for my products and services?' sit right at the heart of customer planning. Ignore these and myths like #4 about recouping today's discount on the next deal can come back to bite.

Every turn he took in his increasingly frantic search for the exit was met with a blockade of evergreen. There appeared to be no going back, but nor did there appear to be any way out.

The People element is central in a high-performance selling organisation. Myths about needing a sales person urgently (Myth #10) and your sales team giving you honest feedback if something's going wrong (Myth #5) are real beliefs in some quarters. Muttered in hushed tones beside the coffee machine, they linger seditiously, waiting for the opportune moment to trip us up.

Tiny, twitching, searching. Indiscernible in the dark they gathered pace as though scenting their prey. And then they began to twine and twist. Around him.

Prioritise the key people measures, though, and your organisation looks and feels completely different. Chapters 22–27, about sales people and creating a healthy sales culture, provide answers on how to achieve the victories that will set you on the road to a truly buzzing business.

Finally, but by no means least, is Do: the action that pulls it all together.

Not convinced? Two thousand years after his death, Emperor Hadrian is remembered in this country for his failure to subjugate the Scots. His wall marks the point where the greatest empire of its time could no longer get the job done on the ground. It's all in the implementation. The myth that customers are sales' job (Myth #14) and that the CRM system will reveal all (Myth #12) allow the Roman legionnaires to sit around the fire moaning. Bust those myths by focusing on topics like building an efficient sales funnel and learning how to prove the return on your investments.

Why does it take all three to build a sustainable sales capability?

Plan and Do is the default sales approach. That's assuming you plan. Creating a strategy, aligning objectives and targets and expecting the team to run off and deliver results is almost the de facto way of running a sales team. And within reason, it works.

The shortcomings of this approach might only be noticed when you realise that marketing isn't dancing to the same tune as sales, or your finance director doesn't think the sales team is good value. Different cultures. Trust can also be a major casualty.

Remember sales KPIs in Myth #8? Plan and People is the approach taken by many large organisations. There's a structured (and well-paid) hierarchy of decision-makers that ensures nothing gets signed off without senior intervention. Annual plans are scrutinised and filtered through a range of sign-off meetings. Nobody wants to be the one who steps out of line.

In one real-world example we saw a sales person struggling to force through a piece of new business that stood to make his business £30,000 for an investment of just £1,000. This seemingly simple decision needed seven signatures for approval and took six weeks.

The shortcomings of relying on just Plan and People are shown in the rapid rise of disruptor businesses in recent years. The UK has almost six million small businesses,[32] many of whom are carving out a niche for themselves by being more focused or more agile than larger, more established competitors. The problem many large organisations have is simply in dedicating enough people to get the job done.

Finally, People and Do is another combination that misses a crucial ingredient. It's one that's not often seen in business, as directors rarely focus on People at

32 'Composition of the 2019 business population' (department for Business, Energy and Industrial Strategy, updated 2020), www.gov. uk/government/publications/business-population-estimates-2019/ business-population-estimates-for-the-uk-and-regions-2019-statistical-release-html, accessed 14 January 2021

the expense of delivering the Plan. Numbers are likely to trump the 'fluffy stuff'. You might find a client who works like this though, especially if you're dealing with non-commercial organisations like government (think NHS, education) or charities.

The really positive news is that by running your business to include Plan, People and Do, you can achieve results that are multiplied by a factor of three. It might not be magic, but it's a powerful potion.

Everything within his business was totally intertwined – he saw that now and he didn't know what to change for fear of making things much worse.

Plan. People. Do. Where should we start? It's a frequently asked question. If you want to complete an MBA you'd start with strategy (Plan). Begin with what you want to achieve, how you think you can best do that and align people and financial resources accordingly.

Meanwhile in the real world... Business is moving quickly, and in most industries, we don't have a nine-month programme to decide what to prioritise. The reality is that we're constantly revisiting the Plan, People, Do principles – evaluating each of them on a frequent basis to ensure that our people are happy and efficient, the plan is happening, and it's all done with an eye on where we want to end up.

This is why you should be wary of the sales fairy.

The 'proven to double your business', radically different new sales approach that has delivered success Everywhere – with a capital E.

Plenty of consultants and sales people will quickly jump to the suggestion posed by the client (sales training, better CRM system, DiSC personality profiling…) and attempt to close the sale. When you're busy it's so tempting to lavish hard-earned cash on these quick wins, packaged as they are to promise easy results.

'Plan, People, Do' helps to unpick these one-dimensional promises and explore what's best for the business. You might ask for sales training, but without the right quality of leads coming into the sales team, the coaching capability to reinforce it back in the day job or a culture that allows a couple of mistakes, training won't work. It will waste time, money and hope.

An upgrade to your CRM contract might promise higher conversion rates and accelerated repeat rates, but without the motivation to capture the right data, the skills in the team to foster customer relationships and the knowledge of the KPIs that truly drive the business, it won't add what you think. More time. More money. Less hope.

The pragmatic response to where to start is that the prompt to change can come from anywhere. Whether it's Plan, People or Do doesn't matter. The first and really encouraging step is that you know you want to start at all. Many people will just slog along, dissatisfied with results, second-guessing which way to turn next.

He paid no attention to the gentle tickle on his neck as he scanned about in the darkness trying to work out what next. Nor did he notice what was happening at his feet.

Above all else, begin with the customer. From here you can shape business plans that are a combination of Plan, People and Do. They won't be neatly broken into thirds with each taking 33% of effort. Prioritising customers will take more planning than onboarding – but each activity is most effective when Plan, People and Do are combined. Adopt this mentality regularly and you can confidently anticipate the final triumvirate: Sustainable. Sales. Growth.

Someone had shown up with a chainsaw and punched a hole in the maze.

Scrambling out, he looked back at his route and realised the maze wasn't for him alone. Sure, some people carried a route-map and others employed a full team of gardeners, but some he'd known for years remained trapped inside, unsure of their path.

He set his eyes on the horizon and marched into the sunshine.

Acknowledgements

There are three groups of people without whom this book wouldn't have been possible.

Firstly, the countless friends we've made during our sales careers, so many of whom have generously shared their wisdom and experience to help us along the way. The resilience and humour of these sales people is what keeps sales teams ticking, and ensures that even the most challenging days contain something to smile about.

Secondly, our hats off to those sales managers and directors who've taken inexperienced and overconfident young people and moulded them into sales professionals, entrusting their company's reputation to people with so much to learn. Without you taking a chance on us none of this would have happened. Here's to the next generation of managers doing more of the same.

Finally, our customers and clients, for sharing with us their goals and plans and for trusting us with their dreams. Their continuing quest for smarter methods of selling and better ways of building sales capability is what keeps us on our toes and nudges us out of bed each morning.

Thank you all.

The Authors

M artin and Lynne are a husband-and-wife team who co-founded Sales: Untangled® with the vision of helping overloaded small business owners love sales.

Lynne Kennedy

Gardener. Hiker. Explorer.

A native of Sunderland, Lynne worked for international businesses including Mars, Boots and De La Rue before setting up her own business two decades ago.

Her expertise is sales training, coaching and sales consulting. With an instinct for business relationships she can unpick tangled teams and processes, rewiring the business in a way that motivates individuals and inspires improved performance.

She specialises in story-telling, people and pictures and is invariably accompanied by Haribo and cups of tea.

Martin Knowles

Cyclist. Pianist. Traveller.

Growing up in Hull, Martin has held senior sales positions in consumer organisations such as PepsiCo, Reckitt Benckiser and the BBC and healthcare businesses including GlaxoSmithKline, Novartis and Sanofi.

He obsesses about customers and consumers and helps focus businesses on maximising value from their key customer relationships.

Martin emphasises the collaboration between supplier and customer that delivers value beyond just the financial results. He's the driving force behind Sales: Untangled® becoming a certified B Corporation.

Contact

For further sales resources and upcoming Sales: Untangled® events visit salesuntangled.co.uk/ untangle-your-sales or contact us via LinkedIn:

Lynne Kennedy: www.linkedin.com/in/ lynnekennedysalesuntangled

Martin Knowles: www.linkedin.com/in/ martinknowles